PARENTS

PARENTS

The Jaw-Dropping, Self-Indulgent,
and Occasionally Rage-Inducing World
of Parent Overshare

BLAIR KOENIG

A Perigee Book

A PERIGEE BOOK
Published by the Penguin Group
Penguin Group (USA) Inc.
375 Hudson Street, New York, New York 10014, USA

USA | Canada | UK | Ireland | Australia | New Zealand | India | South Africa | China

Penguin Books Ltd., Registered Offices: 80 Strand, London WC2R 0RL, England
For more information about the Penguin Group, visit penguin.com.

STFU, PARENTS

ISBN: 978-0-399-15976-3

An application to register this book for cataloging has been submitted to the Library of Congress.

First edition: April 2013

PRINTED IN THE UNITED STATES OF AMERICA

10   9   8   7   6   5   4   3   2   1

Text design by Tiffany Estreicher

While the author has made every effort to provide accurate telephone numbers, Internet addresses, and
other contact information at the time of publication, neither the publisher nor the author assumes any
responsibility for errors, or for changes that occur after publication. Further, the publisher does
not have any control over and does not assume any responsibility for author or third-party
websites or their content.

Most Perigee books are available at special quantity discounts for bulk purchases for sales
promotions, premiums, fund-raising, or educational use. Special books, or book excerpts,
can also be created to fit specific needs. For details, write: Special Markets, Penguin
Group (USA) Inc., 375 Hudson Street, New York, New York 10014.

CONTENTS

STFU PARENTS

INTRODUCTION

After four years of running a website dedicated to mocking and discussing parents "oversharing" about their children on social media, I feel like a bit of a parenting expert. I don't currently have any children, and I don't have a job that involves working with kids or dealing with parents. However, I do have a blog called *STFU, Parents*. (The "STFU" stands for "Shut the Fuck Up," but the content is only occasionally as graphic as the name implies.)

STFU, Parents started the way many blogs do, with a gripe and a dream. As a woman in my late twenties who is active on sites like Facebook and Twitter, I started noticing a shift in my newsfeed content. Suddenly instead of pictures of friends' beer towers, there were pictures of ultrasounds. And instead of updates about a former college roommate's hobbies or career, there were back-to-back posts about naptime and "stinky poo poos." My friends were starting to procreate, at least five years ahead of the time I'll probably have kids myself, and I was overwhelmed by the number of baby updates dominating my computer screen. Was it just me, or was *everyone* experiencing this much kidformation overload whenever they logged in on Facebook?

Between the media, my newsfeed, and the stroller-laden sidewalk outside my apartment in Brooklyn, New York, the subject of parenting was unavoidable. And the coverage was exploding like never before. Now, instead of being vaguely aware of my friends' lives, I was intensely aware of their babies', thanks to a never-ending stream of status updates and photos.

To find out if other people felt the same way I did, I started *STFU, Parents* in March 2009 by posting a screen shot I took of my newsfeed about my friend visiting with her doula. I edited the screen shot to make her name anonymous, and then I posted another screen shot, this time about a baby's fever fluctuations since getting a cold. Word started spreading about the blog almost immediately, and I began receiving submissions from total strangers in my inbox with notes like "I'm so glad I'm not the only person annoyed by these parenting

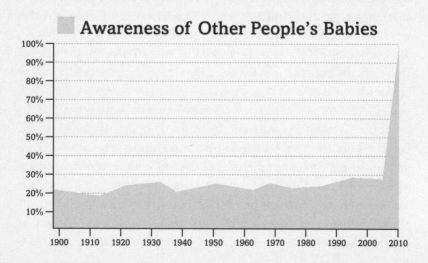

updates!" and "Finally, a place I can vent about my friend who never shuts up about her kids!" As it turned out, people around the whole world were being bombarded by their parent friends' updates just like I was, and some were sharing far more than boring stories about their doula.

From the first day, regular submissions came in and more traffic arrived at the blog. I wrote commentary with all the posts and quickly learned that the term "parent overshare" comprises a lot more than I realized. Pictures of dirty diapers and used training potties were deposited in my inbox with ominous warnings in the email subject headers. "Disgusting Poop Pictures Attached—I'm Sorry!!!" one might say. "Do Not Open While Eating! Nastiest Shit Ever!" another would advise. The more grossed out I got—and the more readers caught a whiff of what I was seeing, as well as my uncensored take on submissions in the commentary—the more the site became a real community. Today, the blog has more than ten thousand daily readers and hundreds of commenters who chime in on each post.

To my surprise, *STFU, Parents* hit the zeitgeist of a phenomenon being discussed in major media outlets surrounding the ways people, and specifically parents, share information in the modern world. Because people have the ability to update their friends and family— a captive audience—about their kids on sites like Facebook, they do. Some post a new picture every day. Others have created Facebook and Twitter accounts for their babies (or fetuses!) and unabashedly post status updates in the "voice" of their infant. As time marched on, I started seeing weirder, and more sanctimonious, examples of parents oversharing, and the blog's audience grew into what it is today: a diverse mix of people ranging from nonparents who want kids someday (like myself) to people who associate with being childfree, to women who have struggled with infertility, to parents themselves.

Of all the audience segments the site has grown, parents have been the greatest. I receive weekly emails from people thanking me for my "public service," saying they use *STFU, Parents* as a "what not to do" guide. It's those emails that inspired this book.

STFU, Parents presents the spectrum of parent overshare offenses, with all the bases covered: Mommyjacking, Sanctimommy, Mama Drama, and Bathroom Behavior. I also discuss topics that seem to bring out oversharing tendencies in parents, such as breast-feeding, parental entitlement, and placenta. And of course, in each chapter, you'll get a look at a different type of overshare in action—guaranteed to make you laugh until you cry or just throw up.

I hope you're entertained by the book, which is sort of like *my* first baby. I'm confident that parents and hopeful parents alike will be able to take away some helpful tips about how and when to announce a baby, whether to post about a child's potty training success, and when to complain about parenthood—versus knowing when to STFU.

Equally important, the book serves as a horrifying bible of sorts for people who wish to remain childfree. After all, what lies within these pages is only further proof that some parents (and their children) are truly obnoxious.

As is the policy on the blog, names and identities have been disguised to protect the innocent (and not so innocent), and as a special treat I didn't include any photo submissions. Regular blog readers know this means you don't have to anticipate any bathtub poop, labor and delivery pictorials, or raw organs chillin' in a bowl, but that doesn't mean this book won't gross you out. It will, and often. I hope you've already eaten, because things are about to get a little crazy.

👎 Five Signs That You Know Parents Who Overshare

- The last five updates your new-parent friend wrote all end with "The joys of parenting!"
- Ever since "The Placenta Smoothie Incident," you no longer eat while checking Facebook.
- When you're scrolling through your newsfeed, you can feel your sex organs shrivel up.
- You know more about your friend's baby's diet than his pediatrician does.
- You catch yourself muttering, "Since when do parents celebrate their kids' half birthdays with cakes that cost more than my monthly mortgage? And why are there 268 photos of the party? What kind of six-month-old needs a bouncy house?!"

1

Alternative Parenting

It's never been easier or more acceptable to be a smug parent with unconventional parenting philosophies. Of course, not all alternative parenting practices are technically "alternative." Some are just old school, like cloth diapering, which everybody did before disposable diapers were invented, or not vaccinating babies before doctors discovered cures for diseases like polio. Man, weren't things *awesome* back then? No one had *time* to think about what constituted being alternative or forward thinking or "normal," since "normal" involved dressing little boys in frilly dresses and potty training babies by the time they could sit up.

Now everyone wants to label parents based on their beliefs, and some parents will go out of their way to *tell* you their beliefs. In my opinion, those are the real alternative parents. Like an alt-rock band from the '90s, these parents are trying hard to be different and, in some cases, flaunt their philosophies as an act of superiority.

One thing alternative parents are totally cool with is technology. They happily tune into Facebook and other social media sites with the rest of the world, and they blog and enjoy a connected life. They may not have as much time to play Farmville in-between unschooling their kids and making birth art out of clay, urine, and love, but they manage to find time to post updates here and there.

Jessica who knew you could gain such utter satisfaction laundering cloth diapers?

about an hour ago • Like • Comment

👍 **Anne-Marie** likes this.

> **Hannah** seriously! i feel like i'm saving the world every single time! :)
>
> about an hour ago • Like

Here's the thing with cloth diapers: They are not nature's answer to shitting. Yes, they are better for the environment in that they're not sitting in giant piles of slowly decomposing waste in landfills. And yes, they are much cheaper, since you wash and reuse them rather than throw them out the second they get wet. But people who use cloth diapers still have to *clean* those cloth diapers, using this precious liquid called water, which means that technically, they still have an impact on the planet. They're great answers to an expensive and smelly problem, but they're not "saving the world one bowel movement at a time."

Let's all just be thankful that we're no longer slinging our poop from pots out of three-story apartment windows, okay?

Brenda hasn't had a poopy diaper at home in weeks! I love ECing!!! ♥

4 hours ago • Like • Comment

👍 **4 people** like this.

John ?

3 hours ago • Like

Brenda Elimination Communication! I know when she's pooping (she cues me) so I stick her on the potty!

3 hours ago • Like

Taylor Sweet!!!

3 hours ago • Like

Shannon That's awesome!

3 hours ago • Like

Sara How does she cue you? What does she do? Very rarely do I know if Madison poops/pees. She is showing no signs of being potty trained anytime soon. :(

2 hours ago • Like

Brenda She catches my eye and goes Mom! Looks focused and grunts a little. I get a couple mins warning.

2 hours ago • Like

Sara Man I wish I was that lucky. I just got stinky poops. Lmao.

2 hours ago • Like

If you've ever thought it was weird to add a heart to a status update about something unconventional that you love—such as gardening nude, flossing, or paying weekly visits to a wax museum—then now's the time to do it. Don't be shy! Express yourself, either by posting on social media or by communicating through a series of telling grunts.

Hollie i SQUATTED on the bed for braeden's birth, with the support bar, OPENING my pelvic outlet, instead of laying flat on my back with my knees and feet in the air, pushing AGAINST GRAVITY. and he JUST SLID ON OUT (ok, with me urging brian to get him out get him out. but thankfully brian, nor my CNMidwife, pulled on his head). mamas, GET OFF YOUR BACKS . . .

2 minutes ago • Like • Comment

> **Hollie** and now i'm reliving (in my mind) that GLORIOUS AMAZING BIRTH!!!!!!!! BEST BIRTH EVER!!!!!!
>
> 2 seconds ago • Like

I'm all about women taking pride in their babies' natural births, but what I don't need is to read a sermon peppered with scary capitalized words like "OPENING," "AGAINST GRAVITY," and "JUST SLID ON OUT." If you feel the need to YELL AT ME about LABOR AND DELIVERY by talking about your PELVIC OUTLET, you're barking up the wrong tree. And by "tree" I do not mean "birth canal." I just mean stop talking.

Andrea misses her daughter!!! I hate having to share my kids with school! can't wait for her to get home! I don't think I will be able to stop squeezing her!!!

6 hours ago via mobile • Like • Comment

👍 **Brigid** likes this.

> **Carrie** You could do what I do and then you don't have to share! :)
>
> 6 hours ago • Like

> **Marisa** I don't like sharing my kids either :(School is a bummer!
>
> 5 hours ago • Like

For some parents, school is a godsend. It's the first step toward independence, for both the child and the parents, and it teaches kids the importance of time management, self-discipline, and the barter system during lunch. For others, it's a torture chamber meant to keep kids away from their parents.

Who came up with this school mumbo jumbo anyway? Do kids really need to learn about history and math when they could be snuggling at home with their mamas? Do they need to make friends their own age when they already have two best friends in their mom and dad? Here's what I propose: No school until a child feels he or she is ready, and if that means "never" then so be it! We were put on this earth to bond with our parents, not to learn about the Civil War!

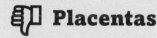 **Placentas**

You may have heard about the not-so-recent trend of mothers incorporating their placentas in everything from hair masks to herbal pills to fruit smoothies, and this section provides a crash course in knowing what all they can be used for. Here are a few ways placentas can be utilized:

PLACENTA AS JERKY

Jade Would have had my Placenta encapsulated had I not ended up in a c-section.

Yesterday at 10:02am • Like • Comment

👍 **Paige** likes this.

> **Meredith** I had mine dried and I ate it. I'd do it again, it turned me into super-mom.
>
> Yesterday at 10:06am • Like 👍 2 people

Jen •gag•

about an hour ago • Like

Meredith There's nothing really gross about it. It looks just like regular meat when it's cooked and you can dry it into jerky or you can dry it and crush it into a powder. I was grossed out when I first heard about it, but it's really not that bad.

39 minutes ago • Like

Jen You know, when I think of a lovely snack, placenta jerky really isn't what springs to mind . . .

25 minutes ago • Like

PLACENTA AS FERTILIZER

Chris Staying home after all. Don't want to leave the boys. I hurt my back earlier too. Planted the placenta under a hibiscus.

21 minutes ago • Like • Comment

👍 **Allen** likes this.

> **Allen** That update rules!
>
> 16 minutes ago • Like

PLACENTA AS ART

Ashley doing a placenta print tonight with Alex . . . very excited!

Yesterday at 12:26pm • Like • Comment

👍 **2 people** like this.

> **Jean** and what is that?
>
> Yesterday at 12:43pm • Like

> **Angela** congratulations . . . so very happy for you 3 . . . :)
>
> Yesterday at 12:47pm • Like

> **Brandy** Um . . . that sounds gross.

Yesterday at 12:52pm • Like

Angela oh . . . about the new addition . . . heehee . . . placenta . . . what the heck is that . . . ? . . . just kidding . . .

Yesterday at 12:55pm • Like

Ashley Well I guess it could be gross, but since it came from my uterus and nourished my babe for ten months it's more beautiful than anything . . . what you do is place your placenta on a flat surface and then smooth a piece of art paper over it and it makes a print with the blood. We'll pick our favorite and frame it. They're lovely!

Yesterday at 1:02pm • Like

Sasha tell us how it turns out!!!

Yesterday at 1:16pm • Like

Jean Wow that sounds really neat :)

Yesterday at 1:17pm • Like

Lauren AMAZING . . . how do you keep it so that it doesn't . . . well . . . decompose? rot? :)

20 hours ago • Like

Scott wow I gotta quit coming on here while eating breakfast . . .

14 hours ago • Like

Brandy Sorry I guess it's my lack of maternal instinct.

13 hours ago • Like

2

Angry Parents

Allow to me begin this section by saying that the only time I feel it's appropriate to use the term *murder* on social media is in relation to food. For example, "I just murdered a burrito," or perhaps, "I'm gonna *kill* some lasagna when I get home tonight!" In other words, I'm of the belief that it's not cool to let out your anger on social media. For one thing, anger is (hopefully) a passing feeling for most people, so holding on to it long enough to type a status update on Facebook is a waste of energy, and aside from that, it makes a person sound crazy.

Still, the mama bears and dadzillas of the world have chosen the Internet as their preferred outlet for expressing hostility over events related to their children, and it's a habit that is sharply on the rise. Blame it on the crappy economy, blame it on reality TV, or just blame it on the fact that nobody gives a shit about anyone else's feelings or opinions anymore, but mama bears and dadzillas seem to be looking for any excuse to go on a rabid threat spree on social media about their problems.

Cassie REALLY gettin fckn sick nd tired of people talkin shit bout what kind if mom I am nd bout what I do w or around him wen u have NO FUCKEN CLUE what ur talkin bout!! Look at ur own fam cuz its HIM thts fckin him up!! Nd don't EVER fckn call someone else my sons mother wen u guys see him fckn TWICE a month!! All a bunch of pieces of shit!!

11 hours ago via mobile • Like • Comment

👍 **Serena** likes this.

Ladies and gentlemen, I'd like to introduce you to the inspiration for the expression "Bitch be crazy." While I appreciate the fact that Cassie spells "piece" correctly (a conscious effort, no doubt), I think it's safe to say someone should revoke her social media license. No one this angry should be allowed to get online. When you start saying things like, "Look at ur own fam cuz its HIM thts fckin him up!!" it's time to put on a Snuggie and say nighty night to Facebook.

Tammy Why do kids think they can be mean to my kids and I'm not gonna go all immature and bite their fucking heads off?

9 minutes ago via mobile • Like • Comment

👍 **2 people** like this.

> **Kim** everyone around here is scared of my kids cause of there momma nothing pisses me off more than fucking with my kids i got to many dam kids for any to be messing with them dam some peoples kids i hate that shit good luck girl
>
> 4 minutes ago • Like

Something tells me if you raided these women's closets you would find a bunch of T-shirts with the following slogans:

"Mess with My Kids and You'll Get Their Mama"
"I Destroy Children with My Canine Teeth"
"Not Afraid to Go Back to Prison"
"I Eat Children for Breakfast"
"Bullies Get the Horns"
"Fool My Kids Once, Shame on Them. Fool My Kids Twice and
    You're Fucking Screwed!"

 Dana got into a fight with a fat child on the playground today because he was harassing my kid. He *might* have been more mature about the situation than I was . . . I did an internal fist pump as I walked away because I *might* have made him cry . . . but you don't mess with Mama Bear's cubs!!

12 minutes ago • Like • Comment

👍 **Rachel** likes this.

> **Kim** Internal fist pump . . . love it!!! You rock mama bear!
> 5 minutes ago • Like

> **Farrah** you crack me up. don't mess with the mama bear!
> 5 minutes ago • Like

Dana is a mama bear who's simply trying to protect her cubs from fat, harassing children who frequent playgrounds when they *should* be at home playing video games and stuffing their fat fucking faces. Who do kids today think they are? It's like they're all out there running around, trying to steal swings from each other on the play-

ground, sticking their tongues out, and generally being disrespect-
ful! Do they think they're going to get away with that behavior
without getting in a little rough-and-tumble with a mama bear?

Mary-Anne all i could think about right now is going out of our front
door to slap our neighbor's daughter silly cause she won't stop
yelling really loud towards this other kid who lives on a different
floor of the same building.

Seriously, if she wakes up Max again (yep, she already did once),
I am going to say a lot of scary sh*t to her so she won't be able to
sleep and she'd cry all night.

3 hours ago • Like • Comment

👍 **7 people** like this.

Listen up, Mary-Anne: One day the kid yelling down the hall is
going to be *your* precious baby bothering the hell out of someone
else, so how about cutting the obnoxious child some slack? I know
what it's like to ~~want to wring high-pitched children's necks~~ feel
annoyed by screaming children, but that's no excuse for acting like
an even bigger brat by threatening to "slap your neighbor's daughter
silly" on the Internet. Seven people "liked" this update, but trust me,
you're crazy.

Emma I have no problem with motorcycles, just drive them carefully!
However, to the person who just wrecked their bike in front of me, IT
SERVED YOU RIGHT!!!! I had my child in the car and you cut me
off!!!!!!

4 hours ago • Like • Comment

👍 **Carly** likes this.

On the highway of life, there are many lessons to be learned. One of them is knowing how to control your rage both on and off the road, as well as on and off the Internet. Based on what Emma's saying here, it sounds like she's got quite a ways to go.

3

Baby 24/7

When people ask me why I started the blog, they usually expect me tell a story about scrolling through my newsfeed and coming across a picture of mustard-colored diarrhea. But the truth is, the inspiration for the site came from a different stream of crap—something I like to call baby minutiae. Baby minutiae doesn't involve bragging or relaying any important information about a child. It's just trivial, boring updates about nothing in particular that parents write on social media out of obsession, boredom, and slight delusion (because they think people actually care about whatever it is their babies are doing that very second). It's probably the most uninteresting category that currently exists on the site, but it's the one that brought me to the idea for the blog in the first place. It's always the little things in life, am I right?

In reality, these little things drive people's friends *crazy*. There are only so many stories that can be told about a baby's giggle, a toddler's love of the letter *S*, or a child's ability to play with a rubber band for two hours straight before shooting it at the family cat. If you're going to post a play-by-play about an afternoon spent at the local pool, at least try to make the updates funny. I'd almost rather see pictures of mustard-colored diarrhea than read thirteen posts about a baby splashing. *Almost.*

Kristen A B C D E F G H I J K L M N O P Q R S T U V W X Y Z
10 hours ago • Like • Comment

Sandra ?
9 hours ago • Like

Kristen Bug is learning the alphabet. N the song is stuck in my head.
8 hours ago • Like

Cool story, Kristen. I feel like I've seen this "alphabet" of which you speak before, but thanks for rehashing the sequence of letters for those of us who may have forgotten. I also like the way you wrote the letter "n" to replace the word "And" in your comment. Was that an intentional celebration of phonetics or just a convenient way of shortening that burdensome three-letter word?

Marcia is watching Nina eat a french fry and go Mmmm!
12 minutes ago via mobile • Like • Comment

The thing about having the ability to update your status as many times as you want on social media is that there wind up being a lot of updates like this one. People's newsfeeds are as clogged with their friends' pointless updates as the average adult's arteries are from eating french fries. The trick isn't for parents to ban themselves from posting about their kids. It's in knowing how to edit which updates make the cut so pages don't get congested with blurbs about all the things a person finds cute or fascinating about a three-year-old. It may not come naturally at first, but no one ever said maintaining a healthy balance was easy.

Teri I put lip gloss on Olivya. It was glittery and now she's got glitter on her face.
Yesterday at 8:56pm via mobile • Like • Comment

This update is the epitome of what baby 24/7 updates are all about. While the story has a clear beginning, middle, and end, the arc doesn't really do anything for me. She put on glittery lip gloss, so now her daughter's face has glitter on it. Wow. Talk about a climax. No picture, no proof, no lip gloss flavor revealed. I guess we'll just have to use our imaginations on that. And what about when Teri went to clean off Olivya's face? There's so much left unsaid, and yet nothing said at all.

Jill applauds Devin for his outstanding pitching today! Only 3 runs scored for the opponents in the first 5 innings! ROCK ON KID! We remain proud of the Braves efforts to play ball at their best! GO BRAVES!!!!!!!!
Tuesday at 12:26pm • Like • Comment

Jill is off to Devin's double header, which excitingly includes another long day into the night at the baseball field. If you're wondering, I do love baseball season INDEED! Hahahaha. GO BRAVES!!!!!!!!!!!!!!!!!!!!!!!!!!!!!!!!!!
Tuesday at 3:42pm • Like • Comment

Jill is SUPER proud of Devin for his triple today and the double play at 3rd! I love seeing him pumped up on the field, and Ben pumped up in the dugout! Tomorrow's agenda? . . . Double header after pictures . . . It's Braves all the way baby!!!

Tuesday at 9:58pm • Like • Comment

Devin's mom exhausts me. I need to toss back a shot of whiskey after reading all of these updates. In fact, I wish I could buy a round for everyone who's taken the time to hear about the Braves. And I don't just mean on Facebook. I'm talking about *everyone* Jill has ever come into contact with, because I have a feeling they've all heard about Devin's "double play at 3rd" and his "outstanding pitching." Jill is the reason the "Hide" feature was invented.

4

Baby Contests

I f you've had accounts on sites like Facebook or Twitter for longer than a day, you're probably familiar with baby contests. Unfortunately these are not contests that determine which baby is the strongest or the most capable of rocking a Tina Turner wig, but instead they focus on which baby is the *cutest*. The prizes range from bragging rights to money to a year's supply of something like air freshener, but that's all beside the point for parents who really just want validation that their child is as cute as they think he or she is.

Sure, in essence I shouldn't care whether someone enters her kid in a dumb contest, and neither should you. Who are we to say that parents can't get a thrill out of voting for their kid by clicking on a picture or hitting the "Like" button? It's harmless! That is, until everyone else's photo is getting clicks and your friend's kid looks like the last one picked for dodgeball.

It's a shitty feeling for a parent to see hundreds of other pictures with dozens of votes while her kid's hovers around seven, all from her and her spouse. And that is precisely when a person goes from, "Hey, this'll be fun!" to, "I will *cut a bitch* if my kid comes in *dead last* in this goddamn contest!" The prize itself matters, kind of, but more than prizes the parents want the glory. They crave attention—attention for their babies—which is what intoxicated them into entering the contest to begin with, and as soon as they realize that, all hell breaks loose. And by "hell" I mean more updates, comments, and messages than you can possibly count for days or even weeks straight reminding people to GO VOTE. VOTE!!!

 Lisa ALRIGHT people. If you haven't already voted for Enos in this photo contest, please DO SO. I've entered him in it so we can win! Don't be lazy . . . Just "like" his picture :)
2 hours ago • Like • Comment

If you haven't voted for Lisa's son, then you are one of the following:

- Lazy
- Selfish
- Forgetful
- Old
- Dead

All of these things are unacceptable. You play to WIN, people. Lisa didn't enter her kid in this contest to embarrass herself, so get on the ball. :)

Monique This weather makes me wish it was 90+ out and summer. I can't wait to go to the lake and just feel the warmth on my skin!

36 minutes ago via mobile • Like • Comment

👍 **4 people** like this.

> **Donna** can you vote on our pic
>
> 21 minutes ago • Like

Donna has gone from "friend" status to "bot" status. Her contest stamina has exceeded her brain capacity and turned her into a totally mechanic, mommyjacking robot, and there's no telling when she'll return to her old self. If her kid wins this contest, she may never come back. (But she'll take some *great* Christmas card pictures this year with her free camera prize!)

 Heather > Tara Please like Kacie's picture . . . There's only an hour left and I really need your help to win!

4 minutes ago • Like • Comment

 Heather > Ainslee Please like Kacie's picture . . . There's only an hour left and I really need your help to win!

6 minutes ago • Like • Comment

 Heather > Becca Please like Kacie's picture . . . There's only an hour left and I really need your help to win!

13 minutes ago • Like • Comment

 Heather > Meg Please like Kacie's picture . . . There's only an hour left and I really need your help to win!

14 minutes ago • Like • Comment

Heather > Caryn Please like Kacie's picture . . . There's only an hour left and I really need your help to win!

15 minutes ago • Like • Comment

Heather's tried to contain herself for as long as possible, but now that she's in the final hour of the cute kid contest, *it's on like Donkey Kong*. No friend will go unspammed. No distant relative will fend off her attack. This is a dire situation, and Heather really needs her hundreds of friends' help to win! She's reaching out to literally *everyone* because this is the most important thing happening at this very moment and people must *help her win*. If she doesn't win this contest, who knows what will happen. She sounds like a panhandler begging for dimes on the corner. As sad as it is, those dimes don't usually add up to much.

Rebecca Another day and another chance to vote. Don't let Emersyn down. She is counting on you. And after you vote, please share the page to get your friends and family to vote as well. Thank you in advance for your vote.

Yesterday at 3:42pm • Like • Comment

Rebecca So, I wasn't a math major, but still did well in the subject and the numbers just don't add up. This voting link was sent to 398 "friends" and Emersyn only has 82 votes.

I know some of you have been wonderful and have been voting everyday (thank you SO much and please keep voting), but that also means there is a lot of you that haven't even voted once (that makes me sad).

Please vote as you know I have always voted for you when you asked, joined Farmville, Petville, etc. when you needed me to, and now I need your help. All I am asking is for you to log into Facebook once a day and click the "vote" button on Emersyn's Photo Search page.

Please, please, please click the link in the above messages to vote for Emersyn today and everyday through June 30. If the link doesn't work, search my name as the entry ID.

Thank you.

PS: How am I doing with the Jewish guilt?

about a minute ago • Like • Comment

Ha ha ha, Jewish guilt. Rebecca is so intent on forcing her friends to vote, she's resorted to reminding them of all the huge favors she's done in the past. Farmville requests, Petville, Pirates, etc. She's endured so much. And now all that she is VERY SIMPLY ASKING is that people do one little favor in return. Every day for several days until she fucking says so. How hard is that? Can no one understand basic instructions anymore?

5

Baby Showers

Although baby showers have symbolically existed in some version for thousands of years, no ancient civilization managed to really blow them out into lavish celebrations like we do today. Back then, four-dollar cupcakes weren't even popular, and the parties were more about the arrival of the baby than a showering of gifts for the mother.

Today, women complain that there's not enough expectant mother parking at Target and exchange jokes about cheap strollers while comparing push presents.

One of the most interesting markers of the modern baby shower is the way they're incorporated into a couple's online identity. Until recently, you hoped someone would be kind enough to throw you a shower, or maybe two showers if your mother lives out of state, and you enjoyed lemonade with the girls while opening gifts like cute onesies and sweet little stuffed animals. Today, however, you don't have to wait for people to throw you a shower. You can throw your own goddamn shower, right on the Internet! And you can tell people to buy you stuff, even if half the friends in your six-hundred-person friend list are people you met while playing Mafia Wars. All you have to do is create a baby registry on a variety of websites and then spam the shit out of your friends by sending them constant updates about how much you *need* some of the stuff on that list if people expect you to keep this baby alive once it's born. The reception tends to be akin to that accorded to a bathroom attendant; that is, people avoid you at all costs or just buy your baby a pack of gum because they feel sorry for you, and that cycle repeats until you either start losing friends or give birth.

 Darius If you want to show me and Helen how good of a friend/ family member you really are . . . READ THIS! For those of that don't know, we are having a baby boy. We have registries with Amazon and Walmart . . . all the items in the registry can be sent to our address which is already saved in our registry . . . Buy Us Some Stuff . . . This is our Facebook Baby Shower . . .
27 minutes ago • Like • Comment
👍 **Jason** likes this.

I like the way Darius says this is their "Facebook Baby Shower," as if that's a real thing, like a debutante "coming out" party or a period party. There's nothing more tasteless—or lazier—than throwing yourself an impersonal "shower" on Facebook by posting a link to an Amazon Wish List. What's next? A Kickstarter page for the baby's college tuition?

Lindsay Dear Friends,

I understand that baby clothes are adorable and hard to resist. If you feel that you absolutely MUST purchase clothing for my son, please purchase size 9-12 months or larger, as he has plenty of clothes in every size smaller.

Thank you.

Sincerely,

A new mother drowning in baby clothes

42 minutes ago via mobile • Like • Comment

👍 **5 people** like this.

> **Nora** Sorry I can't make your baby shower but I will get you a gift that I am sure you will like.
>
> 25 minutes ago • Like

Nora better watch it, because Lindsay means fucking business. She does NOT need any more clothes in sizes 0–6 months OR 6–9 months, because apparently e-v-e-r-y-o-n-e on the freaking *planet* shops in those sizes for babies, which is both stupid and obvious. It's like people don't even use their heads when they're looking for quote-unquote "adorable" gifts for a baby. Like they think a baby will stay small forever. Umm, guess what, geniuses? Babies GROW.

Teresa excited for my baby shower today!!!! so glad he is already here so i can drink!!!!!

March 24 at 11:23am • Like • Comment

I can get down with what Teresa is saying, because after months of carrying a baby, it's nice to be able to relax and have a drink. But I'm not sure it should be like a multiple-exclamation-points type of drink, right? That takes things from "a couple of cocktails" to "I'm claiming my own fishbowl." Even if you *are* planning on getting hammered on mimosas and spiked lemonade at your baby shower, I don't know if you should announce it online. It's sort of like saying, "Excited about getting my wisdom teeth removed so I can stay loaded on Vicodin for several days!" You don't need to *say* it. You just do it.

Kelly Thinking about planning my own baby shower. Feeling like I'm the only one who cares about it.

30 minutes ago via mobile • Like • Comment

> **Meaghan** Stop being such a crabapple.
>
> 27 minutes ago • Like

> **Kelly** Nothing is being done.
>
> 25 minutes ago • Like

> **Meaghan** Stop worrying about it.
>
> 24 minutes ago • Like

> **Kelly** I will stop worrying when things start moving forwards instead of backwards.
>
> 21 minutes ago • Like

> **Meaghan** Showers aren't mandatory. I never had one.
>
> 19 minutes ago • Like

> **Kelly** People said they wanted through one for me but now it doesn't seem important anymore. So I will either plan it or people can just send me stuff.
>
> 18 minutes ago • Like

> **Meaghan** Act like that and nobody will want to throw you one. People will send you stuff anyway.
>
> 15 minutes ago • Like

Kelly I'm just frustrated with it all.

14 minutes ago • Like

Arielle I'm pretty sure we have started doing stuff but if you'd like to do it yourself let me know.

12 minutes ago • Like

Remember, ladies, just because you're hormonal and pregnant and totally capable of breaking anyone who gets in your way in half, you can't force anyone to do anything for you. And you certainly can't force anyone to purchase anything for you. No matter what happens with your shower, try not to have a public meltdown. No one will ever forget it.

6

Bathroom Behavior

Ever since starting *STFU, Parents*, I've received several emails a week that begin, "I read the GROSSEST status update about projectile poop and instantly thought of you," or, "Check out this horrific picture of a child covered in diarrhea. I knew I had to send it to you!" While I think it's lovely that people read about human excrement and think of me, it's also a little disconcerting.

At the time I started the blog, I was just irked by my friends' nonstop updates about their baby's fever or the occasional off-putting maternity picture. I had no idea that there are sick bastards who post in great detail about their kids' bathroom behavior on their Facebook page. If someone had sat me down on that fateful day that I decided to start a "light and funny" blog and said, "You are about to have VIP access to the finest collection of 'shit lit' this side of China!" I'm not so sure I would have signed up for the gig.

But now here we are, thousands of poo-splattered submissions later, and I can practically eat a cheeseburger while going through my inbox. If I was a mom I'd say, "You know you're a mom when you can organize a latrine's worth of poop status updates while eating a burrito and watching *The Bachelor*!" Except, I'm not a mom. I'm a writer who fears the day that her computer breaks and must be taken to the repair shop, awaiting wide-eyed disgust from an Apple Genius Bar nerd who comes face-to-face with what appears to be a bizarre and disturbing fecal fetish.

 Maggie Loves when her son climbs in bed with her right after he peed his own bed & wants to cuddle! Mmmhm like takin a nice warm bath!

5 hours ago via mobile • Like • Comment

👍 **Karen** like this.

> **Jessie** Yuck!
> 20 minutes ago • Like

Maggie's joking, right? By adding "mmmhm" to a status update about her son pissing all over her in bed? I think this is one of those "had to be there" moments. I also think that if I *had* been there, I would have immediately left the room.

 Meredith Bella had a stinker today. I was sitting on my moms bed with Bella in front of me. I opened up her diaper and she squirt, yes squirt, poop from her butt all over me and my moms bed. I was dripping poop. How gross it that?

4 hours ago via mobile • Like • Comment

> **Bess** totally has happened to us before. I freaked out. it is so gross because it isn't normal poop it is disgusting baby poop. I really want to see him. I bet she is adorable. all ur kids are :)
> 4 hours ago • Like

Despite the graphic description of Meredith's baby squirting poop "from her butt" (as opposed to some other orifice?), I'm slightly amused by Bess's comment. From the distinction made between "normal poop" and "disgusting baby poop" to the confusingly goofy "all ur kids are :)," she wins my vote for most resilient poop commenter.

 Jake Violet is still suffering with constipation, she just can't pass her poo poo's . . . ! :o(
3 hours ago via mobile • Like • Comment

> **Robin** Fig dates currants pure orange juice anything that will pass straight through have to with Marley sometimes Marley has curry sauce too mild kinda spicy she loves it but keeps the balance cuz she loves cheese which blocks her up
> 3 hours ago • Like

> **Jake** Violet is struggling to pass a huge poo, her poor bum is stretched to the limit and its to painfull for her to push it out . . .
> 3 hours ago • Like

> **Robin** I know but if you give her something that is gonna go straight through then it will change it it will make it easier for her cuz the poop will just change to gloop
> 3 hours ago • Like

". . . cuz the poop will just change to gloop." I dare you to erase that rhyme from your memory. Also, it's ironic that Jake and Robin are discussing constipation, because it appears their sentences both have *the runs*. Get it?! Because they can't use proper punctuation?

Sorry, I'll stop now.

Dan Have you ever had to physically pull poop out of a kid as they're screaming? Yeah that just happened.

Saturday at 12:17pm via mobile • Like • Comment

> **Susan** Dan? I'm not judging, here—I've never been a parent—but I just have to say, if you ever tried to pull poop out of me, I'd scream too. I'm sure it would be a scarring experience for both of us. :-(Hope yours and the little one's day gets better!
>
> Saturday at 12:26pm • Like

> **Dixie** Your excellent adventures with poop are only getting started, my friend. Have fun with that.
>
> Saturday at 12:27pm • Like

> **Bonnie** Yes. It is awful. Miralax works wonders.
>
> Saturday at 12:42pm • Like

> **Mike** that's love.
>
> Saturday at 2:57pm • Like

> **John** wow . . . can't say that I have . . .
>
> Saturday at 6:07pm • Like

> **Matt** Had four of 'em, Dan, never saw that. I hope you wore a glove or something.
>
> Saturday at 7:11pm • Like

> **Dan** Haha thanks for all the comments, I'm now able to look back on this traumatic experience and laugh.
>
> Saturday at 8:18pm • Like

It's nice that Dan is able to look back on this experience and laugh, but I sure as hell won't be laughing for *a while*. I'm not saying that "pulling poop out of a kid" is wrong. As a parent you *doo* what you've got to *doo*. But talking about it online, no matter how many of your friends with young children are going through the same thing, is WRONG. I'm just glad there's no video evidence. And I hope Dan ~~amputated~~ washed his hands before typing this update.

 Laura was so excited the past two days Britney has had no accidents and has kept her underwear dry all day! today we had our first poop in the potty which was so exciting (oh the life of a mother lol) then a few hours later she took the biggest poop i have ever seen come out of someone so small unfortunately it was not amazing as it was all in the underwear . . . two steps forward and a giant crap back haha

4 hours ago via mobile • Like • Comment

👍 **Haley and 12 others** like this.

> **Courtney** TMI hun ;-)
> 4 hours ago • Like
>
> **Laura** haha sorry
> 4 hours ago • Like
>
> **Laura** everyone else tmi on here too so i thought i would go there like everyone else haha
> 4 hours ago • Like
>
> **Courtney** I was good til about halfway through.
> 4 hours ago • Like

Just like you shouldn't jump off a bridge just because everyone else is doing it, you shouldn't post about potty training or go into detail about your daughter's shitting habits just because everyone else is "TMI'ing." That's when your inner voice is supposed to kick in and say, "These people are undignified, and I will never be like them," and not, "What the hell?! If other parents get to post about their kids potty training, then I want to, too!!!"

 Julie discovered this morning that her Smucker's natural peanut butter is the same color, texture and consistency as her daughter's natural poo poo. Lesson Learned. NEVER forget to wash your hands.

20 minutes ago • Like • Comment

👍 **5 people** like this.

Is anything more disgusting than a status update about eating human crap off your hands? How about one that directly compares your friend's daughter's "poo poo" to a delicious snack typically spread on bread or spooned directly into one's mouth? That'll do the trick.

7

Boy Parts TMI

I t's hard to believe that just a few years ago I didn't know much about baby penises. Call me a late bloomer, but I just wasn't knowledgeable about things like circumcision, swollen balls, and baby boners. In fact, according to most of the submissions I receive, most parents weren't either, which is surprising to me because I assumed that stuff would be covered in the five gazillion baby books on the market. But apparently it's not. Parents are so taken aback by the shock of these things—particularly the "standing at full attention" aspect—they can't help but feel a wave of surprise and discomfort and pride all at once. They're shocked that their little mister's little mister is so "present" and capable of weird, bulbous things at such a young age.

While I understand why some parents feel inclined to share this private information about their son's manhood on sites like Facebook, I never understand why they actually *do*. For one thing, it's awkward, and for another, it's *incredibly fucking awkward*. No one's friends should know details about their baby's genitals via Internet updates, and no boy parts should ever be discussed online, period. If there's something wrong with a baby's penis, call a doctor. If not, and you still feel like discussing it, call a shrink. Either way, don't talk about it on social media, because no matter what the exact percentage is, there's a guarantee that more than half of a person's friends will not approve or find it amusing.

 Jennifer Why do men like when women touch their balls? Every diaper change, Tad smiles as big as he can and sometimes laughs when his balls get wiped. He has now pooped a record number of times today and I think he is doing it just so I have to touch his baby balls.

17 hours ago • Like • Comment

👍 **3 people** like this.

> **Mark** Do you really want an answer to this?
> 16 hours ago • Like

> **Jennifer** really do! I am expecting some fantastic replies from my favorite buds.
> 16 hours ago • Like

> **Mark** I'll keep it simple: Because it feels great!
> 16 hours ago • Like

Obviously the dude in this exchange is preaching to the choir, but I feel there's no way Jennifer wasn't at least partially baiting him with her incredulity. Is she really trying to convince her friends that she has no idea why her son likes his balls being fondled when she's cleaning them off? I don't understand how that works. Is this like her poker face? Or does she sincerely not understand that balls are sensitive because of nerve endings and whatnot? Either way, I'm sufficiently weirded out.

 Gwen My son had a HUGE surprise for me yesterday morning and I can Not get the image out of my head . . . little boys should come with warning labels because I was so not prepared for that!!!
4 hours ago • Like • Comment

> **Charlotte** O_o i'm scared to ask . . . but feel like u should share for the rest of us who may have little boys one day
> 4 hours ago • Like

> **Gwen** Two words: Morning. Wood.
> 4 hours ago • Like

> **Charlotte** O_O i.can't.
> 4 hours ago • Like

Two words: Penis. Update.

Two more words: Not. Cool.

I'm pretty sure little boys *do* come with warning labels. They're called baby books. Also: Google.

 Sean It feels a little weird cleaning Brantley's weiner . . . then I realized why. It's the only weiner besides my own that I've ever handled. I hope it doesn't scar him for life.
52 minutes ago • Like • Comment

> **Kathy** I feel weird just reading this . . .
> 45 minutes ago • Like

> **Sean** Yeah, this was probably an inappropriate overshare.
> 36 minutes ago • Like

Kathy Haha!

31 minutes ago • Like

At least Sean can recognize overshare as he's doing it. I feel as though he's maturing before our very eyes. With any luck, he won't be sharing potty pictures when Brantley gets a little older. Although I must say, if Sean doesn't already have a habit of oversharing, this was taking quite a leap from sports and politics.

 Brianna Gavin's got waterballs?! Lmao Gavin's weird :)

9 hours ago • Like • Comment

> **Suzanne** do i even WANNA know? Don't answer that even . . . hehe
>
> 9 hours ago • Like

> **Brianna** Gavin went to the dr today and he has a hydro seal so his scrotum is filled up with liquid so it's swelled up a little bit lol it's weird.
>
> 9 hours ago • Like

There's no nice way to say, "Please leave your son's liquid-filled scrotum out of my newsfeed." Nothing is "lmao" or "lol" about swollen testicles floating in "liquid." Might I suggest this mother hydro-seal her mouth shut? Her son may only be a baby, but he and his scrotum have feelings, too.

8

Breastfeeding

Breastfeeding is one of those subjects that will probably be discussed on social media forever. The women of the La Leche League have made it their mission to make breastfeeding a top-of-mind topic that shan't be ignored by the masses, and that's including Internet audiences on social sharing sites. They want the world to embrace breastfeeding for its health and bonding benefits, and they want nay, *demand!*—the public to become more comfortable with the sight of a mother nursing to nourish her baby.

And that's the part where things get a little sticky for me. The thing is, as much as I believe in the power of change through beating people over the head, there's a time and a place to make a statement about breast milk and societal norms and patriarchy. As much as I understand why nursing mothers have come together on heavily populated social networking sites to gain exposure, so to speak, I'm not sure it's ever okay to appropriate something and use it against its intended purpose to an almost militant degree. Sometimes the breastfeeding war engaged by women on Facebook can feel like a hostile takeover, and for people who just want to catch up with their friends and click on recommended videos of yawning kittens, that doesn't fit the bill. I'm not saying women should withhold their viewpoints in favor of one or even a hundred people's ignorance or dissent, but I think it's fair to say that people would be content not reading about their friends' chafed boobs as they're surfing their newsfeed at work.

 Cheryl No coffee creamer? No worries! Cheryl's yummy boob milk to the rescue. Sweet n nutritious coming to a dairy near you ;)
2 minutes ago • Like • Comment

Step right up! Who would like to be the first person to sample the goods from this here sustenance provider? Sweet 'n' nutritious, coming to a milkshake near you! Don't knock it till you try it, folks. This stuff is yummy!

 Tiffany So I have found out that I have a breast yeast infection. It is the worst thing ever. My girls have been on fire for 7 ½ weeks now. I guess it's a pretty hard thing to heal too, so tomorrow I am meeting with the lactation nurse to help me dry up.
3 hours ago • Like • Comment

Hope Wow TMI? Hope it gets better.
3 hours ago • Like 👍 1 person

For those of you who don't know, women deal with crazy shit with their breasts once they get pregnant. And a lot of women will tell you that a breast infection is worse than any pain they've ever felt. I'm sure it's difficult not to discuss when you're out, say, walking the dog or picking up a prescription. But if you feel the need to share the information online, do it in the form of an email to specific friends who might actually be able to offer up advice. By posting it on social media, you're basically no different from a person talking about having a vaginal yeast infection, which I think we can all agree is equally TMI. If it involves the word "yeast" and a body part, don't write about it on social media. That rule also applies to using the words "cottage cheese."

Brooke My son is a lively eater. He will take himself off the buffet to chat with me, and then return to eating. Takes longer, but I wouldn't have it any other way.

about an hour ago • Like • Comment

👍 **5 people** like this.

> **Jeanne** This gives you a preview of your son at the dinner table later in his life. Very sociable little gentleman.
>
> about an hour ago • Like

Really, Jeanne? Is that the preview Brooke's son is giving her? That he's going to pull out a woman's chair for her, compliment her on her dress, and pick up the tab at the end of the meal? You can glean all of that from the fact that he "takes himself off the buffet to chat," that is, make gurgling noises like a baby? If there is a study on this I'm interested in seeing it, because from where I'm sitting it sounds like bullshit.

Anna I am so talented I can pump and drive at the same time!!! Mother's are pretty awesome and fierce!

about an hour ago • Like • Comment

👍 **2 people** like this.

Caitlin i think there are laws against that. you can text too. haha
3 hours ago • Like

Eden Oh my, pump & drive . . . . just doesn't sound
right . . . .
3 hours ago • Like

Amelia Lol.. Its so funny u posted that cuz I was just doin the
same thing yesterday!!! Sometimes us busy mothers just gotta
do what we gotta do!!!
2 hours ago • Like

Did you hear that? Super Mom can do it all! It doesn't matter if it's legal because DUH, she's Super Mom! Did Superman ask for permission before flying across the solar system to stop meteors from hitting the Earth? Did Spider-Man send a letter to building owners before scaling their walls? I don't think so, people! Super Moms are perfectly capable of pumping milk from their breasts and driving at the same time *because they say so!* It's called "multitasking," and anyone who's ever had a baby knows that it's what a woman's body is meant to do! Women were not built to confine their breasts when they're leaking; their bodies were built in such a way to accommodate pumping *and* driving *and* listening to the radio all while drinking a diet soda and making a grocery list in her mind. That's the way God made a woman, and no cop is gonna tell her otherwise! Unless of course he pulls her over and writes her a ticket. Then I suppose all that Super Mom stuff goes out the window along with her license and registration.

9

Dr. Mom

"D r. Mom" used to refer to the fact that moms wear many hats. It was sort of tongue-in-cheek for mothers to say stuff like, "I kiss boo-boos and bandage bruises and antisepticize scrapes when my kid falls, so I'm Dr. Mom!" Dr. Mom knew which cartoon-themed Band-Aid her child liked the most and that ice cream always makes kids feel better. She had a special touch, aware that vanilla ice cream only mildly relieves pain, while mint chocolate chip sends a kid into a state of ecstasy that erases all memory of falling in a mall fountain.

Today's Dr. Mom is different. Armed with Google and enough baby books to justify a fictitious medical degree, moms truly believe they are capable of diagnosing their children based on their own research. And as long as the ailment pinpointed isn't something like the measles or gonorrhea, they proudly report on social media that their research is more effective than visiting a real doctor. "So it turns out Jazzlyn is allergic to green Jolly Ranchers and that's what caused the rash. Glad I took the time to figure this out without the 'help' of her idiot pediatrician! Score one for moms!"

In a pre-Google world, parents felt confused and occasionally helpless. In a post-Google world, all bets are off. Now all Dr. Mom needs is a lab coat and stethoscope, and boom, she's in business!

 Amy No offense to any nurses out there, but if I leave a message for my son's DOCTOR to call me back, I don't want the nurse with an attitude and no social skills to call me back instead.

about an hour ago • Like • Comment

Hey, all you nurses out there who busted your asses to get through nursing school to become professionally qualified to deal with obnoxious people like Amy: You can take your bad attitudes and lack of social skills and kiss Amy's ass! There's a reason nurses aren't DOCTORS, okay?? And the DOCTOR is the person who needs to be returning phone calls. Patients' orders!

 Joanna Anyway, one of Tenley's eye this evening started to goop up a little. I can't tell if she has a clogged tear duct or if it could be conjunctivitis. At first, the whites of the eye didn't really look pink. I've washed the eye twice with warm, wet cloths and have massaged the duct area of the eye a few times. When I push on the duct area lightly, a whitish goop starts to come out just a little. Also, now the whites of her eyes maybe are looking a little red, just in that one eye. Could it be from me messing with her eye? She's still sleeping a LOT, so her eyes aren't open a lot to tell how red it even is . . . but she's just so little, so I worry.

Any mom advice? Thanks in advance!

13 hours ago • Like • Comment

Summer Are you breastfeeding? If so, express some milk a couple of times a day and put on her eye. A couple of drops in the ear also works for ear infections, and on the bottom for diaper rash . . .

9 hours ago • Like

Breast milk cures everything. Just ask Dr. Mom! No need to go jumping to any conclusions on what's causing a baby's eye to get goopy. First, express some breast milk into the baby's eye a couple of times a day. Then, blow on it gently while humming lullabies and "healing music" like Enya's Greatest Hits. Finally, if her problem hasn't cleared up then consider calling the doctor. But only if you really don't know what it is that's bothering her. Try to figure it out on your own for several days (after consulting your social network of friends, of course), and *then* place a call to the pediatrician's office. Just to be safe!

 Lori Jerrick went to the doctor today . . . My boy is a beast! 75% for height! Wooohooo! Doctor was upset with me for not going with his advice . . . but, I'm smart enough to know, they don't know everything! :)

2 hours ago • Like • Comment

> **Amanda** No they don't!! Mommas ALWAYS know best!! :)
>
> 2 hours ago • Like

> **Sarah** What was their advice??
>
> 2 hours ago • Like

> **Lori** Sarah, he doesn't really care for my ideas on the vaccine schedule.
>
> 2 hours ago • Like

Lori and he wasn't too happy that I rebutted his idea to use bananas as a constipation fixer. I mean, c'mon, I have the internet, I am not a total idiot, you can't just throw pure crap out there just so that you are giving me an answer.

2 hours ago • Like

Sarah Yeah, they just spew stuff sometimes. Or don't listen.

2 hours ago • Like

This is like the Facebook moms version of the 1988 classic "Parents Just Don't Understand" by DJ Jazzy Jeff and the Fresh Prince, except replace "Parents" with "Doctors." Don't doctors realize how smart the average mom is? Maybe back in the 1880s or the 1950s doctors could pull one over on moms, but not anymore! No sirree! Today's moms are what a typical Dr. Mom might call "medically savvy." They don't have doctoral degrees per se, but darn it if they aren't smart as all heck—sometimes proving to be even smarter than the doctors themselves! Especially on a subject like vaccination. If there's one thing moms know about, it's what kind of vaccination schedule to put their babies on, and no doctor is going to convince them otherwise! Sometimes a mother's intuition is worth *two* medical degrees, if you ask Dr. Mom!

Peggy I've finally worked it out. Roseola Infantum. strange how the "first aid for babies" book could tell me, but the doctor couldn't?!

2 hours ago • Like • Comment

Sharon whats that? as long as it works!

2 hours ago • Like

Peggy It's what Paityn has . . . 3 days of Fever followed by a body rash, then it's all over. Not too serious! At least I know now! ;)

2 hours ago • Like

Sharon yay! That's very good news!

about an hour ago • Like

Tracy Doctors don't know everything!!! Sometimes a mothers instincts is all it takes!!!

about an hour ago • Like

Katrina Maddilynn also had that! But her fever was very high and lasted a week. I went to so many docs but none knew . . . Then I Googled the symptoms and treatment, more informative than any doc! The rash will go away in 2-3 days ;(

about an hour ago • Like

Well, isn't this suspicious. Peggy managed to diagnose what was wrong with her child with a *book* all by herself! Excuse me, but isn't this what mothers are paying doctors for? To identify what's wrong with a child? When books and access to the Internet start replacing the need of a doctor, you *know* moms are wising up to the medical field's little game! Doctors don't know everything, that's for sure!

10

Entitled Parents

The sense of entitlement that plagues the Parents of Facebook has hit monstrous levels of douchebaggery. Parents are pissed off about everything. Their kids aren't treated with respect after they misbehave in public places and that is total *bullshit*. Parking spaces are too narrow and parents should NOT have to park farther away from stores because it could rain and their babies could melt. Teachers think they can tell parents that their children are less than perfect and still keep their jobs (paid for by parents' tax dollars, thank you very much!). Worst of all, the world hasn't come to terms with the fact that a small percentage of kids have extreme allergies, and therefore all peanuts and tree nuts should cease to exist. No one seems to get that!

Entitled parents whine and get what they want, which makes sense because their kids whine and are rewarded with the same thing. Most people cater to an entitled mother's demands just to get her off their backs. It's not worth arguing with a woman who begins a complaint by saying, "My baby is a national treasure and deserves to eat a triple scoop banana sundae for free! With sprinkles made of gold flecks!" There's a reason so many baby bans have been set in place, and it's because some parents no longer have any boundaries. If a person so much as looks at a baby the wrong way, there's no telling what entitled and enraged parents are capable of doing. Especially if they have an old diaper buried in their bag, held hostage until the perfect victim comes along on whom to smear it.

Julia Anyone else think that parking lots overaccommodate for disabled drivers rather than parent and child? Seriously, how many disabled drivers are out there?

11 hours ago • Like • Comment

> **Alexis** And I've heard them complain about the parent and child ones being closer to the store . . . Last time I checked it would be unusual for a disabled driver to run out in front of a car . . .
>
> 10 hours ago • Like

Do you know what Julia hates? When people act like there are more disabled drivers out there than there actually are. *Haaaates* that, 'cause think about it: (A) there are probably WAY more parents and children out driving around, and (B) it's not like disabled people are going to run out in front of cars like a little kid might, so why do they need so many spaces right up close to the entrance? No offense to any disabled people out there, but Julia and her child want to park in those spaces!

Abby Fucking old cunts on the bus not moving for strollers!!!! Just wait I'm gonna teach Finn to steal your purses out of your bags!

6 hours ago • Like • Comment

👍 **17 people** like this.

Not only do I get a kick out of geriatrics acting like jerks about a stroller, but I get an even bigger kick out of knowing they messed with just the right person. Sounds to me like Abby needs an attitude adjustment. Maybe she can work on that after teaching her son to steal old ladies' purses out of their bags. There's a reason most people are not fans of large strollers, and it's because some of them are being pushed by women like Abby.

 Mary Dear Old Man Asshole,

Clearly you should not be driving if you need to come to a complete stop at the end of the ramp to get on the expressway. (For NO reason at all.) Please get your license revoked or drive off a cliff so you don't kill the innocent mommies and babies that are behind you and have to slam on the brakes to barely miss you.

Thank you,

Kylie's Mommy

8 hours ago • Like • Comment

> **Colleen** This FU letter is awesome. Yesterday some guy was going 35 on the expressway . . . in the left lane. When I went to pass him he swerved right and I had to drive in the merge lane to avoid him. As we passed I caught a glimpse of his "HEY!! You crazy lady driver" old man squished up face. I smiled and waved. Then thought horrible things about him. I'm sorry some old man driver freaked you and the baby out. Glad y'all are OK.
>
> 8 hours ago • Like

Dear Kylie's Mommy,

Everybody knows that seniors continue driving for much longer than they should because they hate being too old to drive. However, when an old man does something stupid on the road, I recommend yelling out, "Keep it moving, GRANDPA!!! LET'S GO!" while waving your arms up and down, and then continuing about your day. Chill out on the creepy death wishes. Old Man Asshole is someone's loved one, too. You and your baby don't get special treatment just for being a mom and a baby. Sorry.

Thank you, and go drive off a cliff
STFU, Parents

 Priscilla Sooooo for all u people that promised to get my daughter a present for her birth into this world and haven't even tried to see her or meet her, let alone give her her gift, my patients are getting slim! Lol
53 minutes ago • Like • Comment

> **Priscilla** And yes I spelled patience wrong!
> 51 minutes ago • Like

Does it ever occur to parents who say things like this that perhaps their friends just aren't interested in seeing *them*? Because if I was Priscilla's "friend," I don't think my noticeable absence would be due to not wanting to meet her baby. If anything, I'd probably use her daughter as an excuse to not come by. "Yikes, you must be super busy with the new baby. Hope to see you soon!" translates to "You've been a nightmare since you got pregnant. Please get over yourself, then call me and we'll do lunch."

11

Fetuses and Babies Online

Whoever first came up with the idea of creating a social media account for a fetus or baby was on to something. What used to be considered really fucking weird has actually become popular, and yet still no less weird. Perhaps the origins are rooted in sonograms being used as profile pictures for parents-to-be. I can easily imagine a person with a sonogram avatar commenting on her friend's status update and it turning into a strange, confusing joke that "the baby" was talking. Who knows? Maybe the parent-to-be said, "I guess it does look like little Zavier is talking!" and then dashed off to create a new page for the baby, giving birth to a new trend. Sounds plausible.

However it came to be, social media accounts for fetuses and babies have experienced a surge in recent years, with parents using the accounts as a way for their babies to "communicate" their (not yet developed) thoughts. What do babies talk about? Lots of things! Politics, favorite foods, the weather. No subject is off-limits, and it appears most parents want their friends to know that their baby is *very* opinionated on subjects ranging from the new Coldplay album to health-care reform.

Nicole thanks for the playdate Aiden! i enjoyed eating all of your toys. i will not be offended if your mom washes them all before you eat them. love, Kaydee. p.s. how's your squished toe?

26 minutes ago • Like • Comment

> **Whitney** Hahaha squished toe is doing better. Silly mama. The song only says "hands up" not "toes up." What's a baby to do. Thanks for the mum mums and come over for a play date any time. Love your BF Aiden.
>
> about a minute ago via mobile • Like

Here we have two babies talking to each other about a playdate via their social networking accounts. No biggie. They're just chatty babies who immensely enjoy each other's company. There might even be a romance budding between these two! At least, that's what their moms like to say, seeing as they're the ones who are doing the actual talking. They're like mommy ventriloquists!

Bio

Hewwo Dyes! My Name Is Bentley Connor! Iz Just A Wittle Fella Wif A Big Heart! You Tould Say Dat Iz A Chunk! I Wika Waugh And I Wika Cwy! My Paborate Show Is YO GABBA GABBA! You Tould Say Dat Iz A Pamly Man . . . I Wubba Toes Twazy Peoples. I Tank Dat I Wubba To Potty In My Pants Betus I No Know To Doh To Dah Potty In Dah White Seat Tangy. I No Wika Da Doctor, And I No Wika To Doh To Bed. I WEALLY Wika Food, And I Weally

Wika Dah Ladies. Howeber, My Mama Tella Me I No Hab A
Dirlpriend Til Iz At Weast Pourty! But I Wubba My Wittle Wenny!
Her Dah Wub Uh My Wipe! But Enup About a Meah! Whata Bouta
Youah?! :)

Yesterday at 8:27am • Like • Comment

Babies r so funny in der online pwofile bios. Dey luv 2 descwibe their paborate shows on teevee n talk about dey luv 4 food and dah ladies. Dey mamas r so pwoud of dem!

 Beth Dear Little Mommy,

The reason you've been so darn tired the last 2 days is because you forgot your prenatal vitamins that I need so very much yesterday and today.

Love,

your little baby ♥

7 minutes ago via mobile • Like • Comment

> **Paul** it's weird that you're talking to yourself
>
> about a minute ago • Like

Paul is one confused dude. His friend Beth went from being a pretty normal person to a woman who not only talks to herself, but *scolds* herself on Facebook via "letters" from her baby. Baby brain has officially set in and is taking its toll. First she forgot to take her prenatal vitamins, then she got reamed out by her unborn child, and now Paul's got something to say about it?! This baby is becoming such a hassle.

Linzy You're the best Mommy ever. I love you ♥

10:40am • Like • Comment

👍 **6 people** like this.

Corrie I love you too!!!!!

10:41am • Like

Jenny aww lol that's so freakin cute!

10:48am • Like

Linzy :)

10:52am • Like

Molly Yes, you sure do have the best Mommy ever!

11:41am • Like

Jeremy She types damn good for her age!

12:23pm • Like

Corrie I know right!

1:52pm • Like

Haha, Corrie's baby is a damn good typist! Who knew a baby could type so well? Linzy knows how to say "I love you," knows how to type on social media, *and* she knows how to suck up to her mommy! All resourceful skills for a child her age!

12

Gross-Out Factor

Kids are disgusting. They barf, fart, drool, eat their frighteningly huge boogers, and live to tell about all of it (once they can talk, that is). It's kind of crazy that kids manage to be as repulsive as they are and get away with it, but it's because parents are so "in love" with their babies that they selflessly dedicate their lives to making their children as clean and approachable as possible. Parents bonding with their babies over late-night spit up or mid-morning sharts is a beautiful thing, I guess, and I think most people can appreciate the love that goes into that relationship.

That said, when parents post about this stuff on social media, my attitude begins to change. It's like, until people have children, they care (at least, most do) deeply about preserving their image, practicing good hygiene, exercising, and attempting to change their clothes at least once a day. Post-baby, the opposite happens. Parents seemingly "show off" their filth as though they're in the process of earning their parenting merit badges. You'd think people wouldn't be so self-assured, but it's like a contest to see who's got the grosser parenting story. The nastier, the closer a parent is to winning the contest. And there's no better place to watch this dirty competition play out than online.

 Phoebe "Mom, the reason I like to eat my boogers is because in the center of the green part is a little cinnimon spice and it is OOHHH so good! you gotta try this stuff!" lol god I love him!
Yesterday at 4:49pm via mobile • Like • Comment
👍 **5 people** like this.

Wait, I thought little *girls* were made of sugar and spice and everything nice, while little boys were made of snails and puppy dog tails (whatever the hell *that* means). Evidently that nursery rhyme was totally wrong based on the taste of Phoebe's son's boogers. Good to know! Also, why would anyone share this "adorable" anecdote with her entire friends' list? It's disgusting.

 Star Just found a hair stuck between Rhett's buttcheeks!!! Ewww hahaha
9 minutes ago via mobile • Like • Comment

> **Claire** lmao!!
> 6 minutes ago • Like

> **Eric** haha omg thats soo funny!!! at least it was only a hair!
> 4 minutes ago • Like

> **Star** I know right. . . . He kept putting his hands in his diaper and I figured I was gunna find poop . . . But it was mommys hair lmao!!! Bet that was itchy!! Ewwww
> 3 minutes ago • Like

LMAO!!! Hahahahaha!! OMG soo funny! Nothing cracks me up like a good story we can *all* relate to, amirite? Do we not ALL get our mom's hair stuck in our rear ends at some point in our lives? It's practically a rite of passage!

 Russell Our little girl is so cute . . . Even when she sharts!
10:26pm via mobile • Like • Comment
👍 **8 people** like this.

> **Russell** A portmanteau of the word shit and fart.
> 10:31pm • Like

> **Debra** Hahaha you must be so proud :p
> 11:21pm • Like

> **Destiny** I got sharted on this morning while I was putting the diaper back on, hit me right on the arm and all over my shirt!
> 11:24pm • Like

> **Pam** She'll still be sharting when she's 27!!! lol
> 11:39pm • Like

Russell scores points for using the word "portmanteau," but that doesn't give him an excuse for posting about his cute little girl's sharts. In fact, "shart" may be the most nauseating portmanteau in existence, which is why most people don't use it in typical conversation. You never overhear someone at a dinner party saying, "So there I was on a really crowded flight. I'd *just* eaten a bean burrito, and then suddenly WHAM! I'm sharting on the plane!" It just doesn't happen, folks. No matter whose ass a shart came out of, it shouldn't be relayed online.

Stacey first bath success!!! He farts in the tub like his daddy!!

April 27 at 9:04pm via mobile • Like • Comment

👍 **5 people** like this.

 Stacey the noises and faces the baby makes when he poos are so funny!!! however, the smell . . . not so much #likefatherlikeson

April 23 at 12:53am via mobile • Like • Comment

 Stacey I have a poopy, stinky boy!! no, not the hubby (surprisingly)!

April 21 at 5:16pm via mobile • Like • Comment

As they say, the stink of a father's ass doesn't fall far from the tree! Er, wait. That's not right. They don't say that at all. In fact, this father/son comparison is repulsive and insulting. Why is Stacey practically scrapbooking each experience with her son's farts, poo faces, smells, and shit on social media while embarrassing her husband at the same time? This isn't cute; it's nasty.

13

Helicopter Parents

If you've ever watched helicopter parents in action, you know that they're some of the scariest people on the planet. Rather than take each day as it comes and bask in a child's achievements, no matter how small, helicopter parents crack the whip like a stagecoach driver in 1872. Known for "bubble wrapping" their progeny from infancy through adulthood, they're concerned about their children's well-being to an almost paranoid degree. But worst of all, helicopter parents don't really allow their children to do anything for themselves. They want to hold their hand through everything, from potty training to first days of school to first days on the job after college graduation. It's almost like the kids don't ever really grow up, because their parents shelter them and take care of their every need.

It's like the book *I Love You Forever*, in which a mother rocks her baby son to sleep by singing him a lullaby. By the end of the book, the boy is a man rocking his elderly mother in his lap, and it's very sweet, until you consider that this boy's mother was a helicopter parent who snuck into her son's room at night when he was a teenager and rocked him in her lap like some kind of freak.

 Diane Can babies be micro-chipped? They can do it to animals. I'm sure they can do it to humans. I want to get my son micro-chipped when he is born.
10 minutes ago • Like • Comment

It's a little hard to read status updates like this and not think of movies like *The Matrix* and *Total Recall*. Only a helicopter mom (who hasn't even given birth yet) would be thinking of ways to microchip her child so she can know where he is at all times. I'd like to think that Diane is joking, but based on the lack of exclamation points I'm assuming that she's being serious. After all, if we can microchip our dogs and get laser treatments on our eyes, why shouldn't we be able to track every human being on the planet with a basic integrated circuit implant? Sounds like a perfectly good way to assemble human armies before the robots take over, if you ask me!

 Natalie STOP CUSSING ON YOUR STATUS UPDATES, PLEASE!!! Keep it family friendly, especially since Emily is starting to read. Sheesh people . . . get a higher vocabulary. Say something intelligent instead of cursing your head off. RAR! I think I'm just going to have to start hiding people from my feed that cuss.
3 hours ago • Like • Comment
👍 **8 people** like this.

> **Margot** lol, well, i agree (kinda) I've been guilty of that. But, sometimes, you have to express in different words. Good and bad. Some ppl have different the "right" words some people

have the "wrong" words. But you have to also think Facebook is a freedom of expression. So, I'm just trying to put it in liberal terms. Ya know? But I'll clean it up a little more ;)
2 hours ago • Like

Natalie Thanks, I just can't stand cussing in the first place, and having school age kids now, it is that much more important to me. Using foul lamguage just makes the person seem dirty to me. I know there is freedom of speech here, so that's why if people want to cuss, I will just simply delete them from my feed. I won't delete them as a friend, that would be silly, but I really don't want to hop on Facebook to a bunch of cussing rants. It really bums me out. No reason to spread the negativity.
2 hours ago • Like

Margot Definitely :) You'll have to forgive me sometimes, I might be blowing off steam with the wrong words. But thank you for the insight Natalie. :)
2 hours ago • Like

Brandon Natalie, I agree completely.
about hour ago • Like

Theresa aww, man, why you call me out like that? lol, I will try to remember to 'hide' you from those statuses where "darn" and "shoot" won't work!
about an hour ago • Like

Natalie Haha, poor Theresa. There was just one of my friends that was using the F word a lot and it was driving me crazy! I don't mind it so much if you do the whole first letter then asterisks thing . . . as long as Emily can't read/understand it. :)
about an hour ago * Like

It takes a village to raise a child, especially when that child is prone to sitting with her mother as she surfs certain websites, and Natalie's friends need to fucking respect that. Right now, they're acting like giant assholes who don't realize that cussing is for low-minded jerk-offs who don't know how to use the goddamn asterisk button. It's not fucking hard to figure out.

 Elizabeth Ok, I'm about done with Mack's leaf project, Joel helped him collect some leaves and then I did. How come Mack has 2 white walnut leaves (1 from Joel and 1 from me) and neither of them look alike? Really, do you think we can really identify the exact leaf of every tree! Oh, as much as we have I feel like I have been in elementary school for 10 years, you'd think I'd be a pro.

9:54pm • Like • Comment

👍 **2 people** like this.

> **Elizabeth** I'm savin this leaf project for when the twins get in 4th grade. We'll just take Mack's name off and put one of theirs on it! LOL
> 9:54pm • Like 👍 1 person

> **Rosie** I hear ya, I saved Steven's for Harper.
> 9:57pm • Like

> **Jordan** ahhh that is halarious
> 10:01pm • Like

> **Kourtney** Girl thats what I did, I took Dexter's projects and kept them :) I feel you on the homework though, I don't think we ever left school
> 10:04pm • Like

Cameron we finished billy's on monday night and its definately something that will be handed down for the younger ones. I am getting to old to climb trees. LOL

10:15pm • Like

Elizabeth I understand that, its hard to find a good leaf with a drought!

10:19pm • Like

Reading this confuses me. I never realized as a kid that I could have just forced my mom to do all my homework for me, tree climbing and all! I spent so much time collecting my own leaves, looking up their origins in a variety of boring books, and then carefully laying them out in a notebook to turn in to my teacher. Had I known that parents like Elizabeth and Joel were doing all of their children's homework for them, maybe I would have pressed my own a little harder.

Scarlett new muppet movie? awesome.

3 hours ago • Like • Comment

👍 **8 people** like this.

Kristyn I can't take Bradley and Ava. The movie uses the F word.

3 hours ago • Like

Caroline What F word . . . Fuzzy??? Furball? Firetruck?

2 hours ago • Like

Kristyn Eeewww . . . I can't stand to even type it . . . starts with F and rhymes with "smart." I saw the preview and was disgusted.

2 hours ago • Like

Kristyn is appalled and disgusted that Scarlett would even *mention* the latest Muppet movie, much less pay to see it. That movie is garbage with a capital G! She can't even take her small children to see it because of all the profanity. They may be forced to encounter words like . . . well, the word that starts with F and rhymes with "smart" when they're older, but for now Kristyn keeps her children very, very sheltered so they never have to hear such offensive language. And when they do, you'd better believe that Kristyn will make sure they won't repeat the words they hear! Just the other day little Ava called the neighbor's dog "a furry ballsack," and she had to sit in timeout for well over an hour.

14

Holidays

O versharing parents on social media have never met a holiday they couldn't hijack. From Martin Luther King Jr. Day
to New Year's Eve, parents on Facebook manage to find a
way to make any holiday about their kids. Rather than observe or
celebrate the significance of the day, parents consider holidays to be
excellent opportunities to incorporate their children into their status
updates. And I don't mean in the typical ways, like when a parent
posts a picture of her kid on Santa's lap or frolicking at an Easter egg
hunt. I mean by relating holidays to poop, or by using the day as an
excuse to spoil their kids rotten. Social media provides an easy way
for parents to say "Merry Christmas" or "Erin go Bragh" while
sneaking in some quick details about their kids that you probably
didn't want to know. It also provides ample opportunity for some
brazen mommyjacking. What shakes out is a collection of terrible
puns and rants that'll remind you why people so often drink during
holidays.

Cassidy New years eve now officially makes one of my least favorite holidays. How is any one suppose to sleep or keep their baby asleep when fireworks are blazing out your entire house. It sounds like it is hailing with loud pops of sharp thunder continuously! RUDE!

about an hour ago via mobile • Like • Comment

New Year's Eve is a lot like the Fourth of July. People celebrate by making noise later into the evening than usual and parents get very upset and complain about it on the Internet. Around the Fourth, it's easier to understand this attitude because some people *do* treat the holiday like a weeklong excuse to make as much noise as possible, but on New Year's Eve? It's the last day of the year, let's party! Even babies should party! Come on, parents, you can catch up on your sleep later. Like when your child moves out.

Margaret To celebrate Valentine's Day, change your Profile Picture to you and your spouse/sweetheart. Make sure to tell how long you've been together! Copy and paste this to your profile. SHARE THE LOVE!

3 hours ago • Like • Comment

👍 **Kelley** likes this.

> **Amber** We don't celebrate Valentine's Day. Because it is the day my son was born (Lachlan) so we are celebrating his day and you should do the same.
>
> 35 minutes ago • Like

What were you thinking of doing for Valentine's Day? Cooking a romantic dinner? Going on a moonlit stroll with your partner and/ or dog? Well, forget that stuff. Why celebrate a contrived holiday with the same old clichéd activities when you could celebrate a *real* holiday: Lachlan's birthday!

@BabyKaitlyn

In celebration of St. Patrick's Day, my poop was green. Thank you, green beans.

about 10 hours ago

This is a baby posting on his Twitter page about his holiday-themed poop. Talk about the luck of the Irish! Holidays don't get more symbolic than that.

Michelle Just read how someone's kid wanted books on Kindle for Easter instead of chocolate. 1. Stop bragging about your kid. 2. Stop making other kids feel like imbeciles or under-achievers because they want to go Easter egg hunting and gorge on candy. 3. That's not normal for a kid. Chances of your kid being made fun of in school and retaliating by spraying classmates in a school cafeteria is pretty good.

24 minutes ago • Like • Comment

I can't tell if Michelle is attempting to be funny or if she just has it out for kids who like to read. Last time I checked, reading doesn't lead to shooting rampages. It isn't a gateway drug. Just because a kid wants to read books instead of eat candy on Easter doesn't mean he's one biography away from exalting *Mein Kampf*. I'm not saying that people who post about their kids wanting books for Easter aren't bragging—maybe they are—but Michelle is the one who strikes me as being unhinged.

Sheila So my daughter come up to me and says "mommy I pooped" and pulls out brown fingers from the back of her pants. Happy Mothers Day!!!

3 hours ago • Like • Comment

👍 **Melissa** likes this.

> **Nicki** I LOVE it!!!!
>
> 3 hours ago • Like
>
> ---
>
> **Bethany** LMAO—she is so full of it! That's too funny . . . You gotta love it!
>
> 3 hours ago • Like

To be honest, Bethany's comment might gross me out even more than Sheila's original status update. The expression "full of it" is only supposed to imply being "full of shit" *figuratively*. It's not supposed to be in reference to a literally shit-filled situation. Also, I've given it a considerable amount of thought, and there's not a single LMAO thing about Sheila's status.

Elaine 67 years ago today at 6am the greatest generation hit the beaches of Normandy.

about an hour ago via mobile • Like • Comment

👍 **4 people** like this.

> **Christina** totally unrelated—but the girls hit the beach at 7am the last 2 days. New generation and different beaches but much cuteness anyway. Thank you to our soldiers past present and future—so we can enjoy our freedom.
>
> about an hour ago • Like

Perhaps I wouldn't think much of this status update except Christina's comment makes absolutely no sense. Did she really just relate the troops storming Normandy in 1944 to her little girls playing on the beach during their summer vacation? That's a pretty weak analogy. I can't imagine going up to a World War II veteran and saying, "Because you watched your friends die on the beach, my daughters can enjoy *playing* on the beach!" I hope Christina is wearing a hat to protect her precious brain cells while she's seaside.

 Shirley Happy Fathers Day to me cuz my daughters father SUCKS!!!!

4 hours ago • Like • Comment

> **Keri** Don't feel bad, Amie's fathers a piece of shit. hes never seen her.
> 4 hours ago • Like

> **Shirley** Yeah well he lives with me and still acts like a deadbeat
> 4 hours ago • Like

> **Keri** ohh no im sorry hun
> 4 hours ago • Like

> **Shirley** yeah just living miserably
> 4 hours ago • Like

> **Patty** Hey, that's my nephew your talking shit about. He may not be perfect but at least he is taking care of you and Amayah best he can! Some don't give a damn and don't stick around!
> 4 hours ago • Like

> **Shirley** I know auntie hes just overly mean sometimes and in front of Amayah it really isnt necessary
> 4 hours ago • Like

> **Patty** No it's probably not necessary but he's a man and an ass at times like the rest of em but it could be worse. Tell you

what tho if he ever laid a hand on ya me and my sista's will kick his ass.

4 hours ago • Like

Keri Now that's a good auntie looking out for her family!!!

4 hours ago • Like

Patty Thanks Keri!

4 hours ago • Like

Shirley Hes an ass all the time!!!

4 hours ago • Like

Patty LOL

4 hours ago • Like

Oh, aunties. Always the voices of reason. "Don't talk shit about my nephew. He's a good man! But if ever lays a hand on you, I'm gonna kick his ass so hard he'll wish he'd never known me! LOL." Everyone should have an aunt like Aunt Patty.

Lucinda I hate my neighborhood. fireworks until after midnight :(

Yesterday at 12:57pm • Like • Comment

Monica Debbie Downer :(lol

Yesterday at 1:14pm • Like

Leslie i think that was pretty much every neighborhood last night

Yesterday at 1:19pm • Like

Cambra I think our neighborhood was the only one that didn't have fireworks at all. We'll be evicted if we have as much as a sparkler. :(

Yesterday at 1:36pm • Like

Becky Very stressful when you have young ones sleeping. we were sure to run extra fans and a sound machine upstairs. I'm shocked Mylo didn't wake up!

Yesterday at 2:24pm • Like

Kristin Wow . . . we slept thru them all!

Yesterday at 3:21pm • Like

Alyssa OMG, I am so mad because I couldn't sleep. I think they finally stopped around 1am. Then Layla woke me at 5:50.

Yesterday at 4:04pm • Like

Lucinda us too. the kids slept great (fans and sound machines) but were up at 5:45 (yay Chloe) and 7:30. too early after a late night of other people's fun.

Yesterday at 5:42pm • Like

James come on now, remember what it was like when you were young? the 4th is supposed to be loud.

Yesterday at 8:04pm • Like

Lucinda james—talk to me in a few years. you may change your mind

Yesterday at 8:14pm • Like

Try listening to other people shooting off fireworks when you have kids, James! Childless people have no idea what it's like to tolerate such loud noise on a holiday that's *supposed* to be about celebrating America. Not celebrating explosives! They're hostile and they terrify children—children who shouldn't have to sleep with several fans running just to get some rest. Maybe when our babies are a little older and can appreciate and enjoy fireworks we will embrace them, but for now they are very disruptive. And it's not relevant if other children want to shoot them off just because they're at an age where they want to have fun. They should respect all the little babies who are trying to sleep. :(

 Crystal Apparently I picked the wrong costume out for Tasha considering every little girls mother across America has decided to make their child a lady bug..ugh

about an hour ago • Like • Comment

> **Anthony** Lmao! My sis did too
> about an hour ago • Like

> **Danielle** my sister in law has two little girls and they are both lady bugs and i saw several at zoo boo the other night too :(
> about an hour ago • Like

> **Crystal** Well I guess that means I gotta go buy her a new one . . . one my pet peeves is having the same thing as multiple ppl, we like to be different. I thought every little girl would b Dora, princesses n little ponies lol
> 59 minutes ago • Like

> **Jamie** But she will rock that costume like no other!!
> 34 minutes ago • Like

> **Crystal** Oh she def did when I took them to trick or treat at mall. She got soooo many ooooos n ahhhhs n giddy lil smirks of pure joy when seeing my daughter strut n wobble past . . . this is why I am soo saddened by there bein multiple lady bugs . . . it distracts attention from her lol
> 21 minutes ago • Like

"We like to be different and attract as much attention to our baby as possible, so we bought a ladybug costume that came in a bag for

$19.99. Then I noticed that all these *other* kids' mothers had the EXACT SAME IDEA, so now we have to go *back* to the store to buy another costume-in-a-bag for $19.99 because my baby needs to be different! People are going to ooooo n ahhhh n get giddy lil smirks of pure joy no matter *what* she wears when she struts n wobbles past, but we are doing our best to stand out from the crowd lol."

Huh?

Erica HAPPY THANKSGIVING FROM OUR FAMILY TO YOURS :)
Have a wonderful day filled with lots of love & hugs.
Thursday at 7:47am • Like • Comment

> **Erica** BRENDAN WENT POO ON THE BIG BOY POTTY
> TODAY ;) INCREDIBLY AWESOME!
> Thursday at 1:26pm • Like

Happy Thanksgiving from Erica and her family! She hopes everyone has a wonderful day filled with love and hugs and turkey legs and mashed potatoes, and OH YEAH BRENDAN WENT POO ON THE BIG BOY POTTY! Talk about an INCREDIBLY AWESOME day! Now he can finally do what everyone else does on Thanksgiving! Haha! :)

ABOUT AVERY'S XMAS PRESENT—READ ALL :)
by Alicia Monday, November 28, 2011 at 10:42am

Okay, since this is later than I thought, for Avery's xmas gift from family or friends we were asking if everyone could get her at least **ONE** Disney movie, we are building her collection and I will list what we already have so you don't make the mistake of re-purchasing something. If you happen to purchase the same movie as someone else, don't fret! We will just exchange it for something we don't have yet :) Target has $5 movies and Wal-Mart has $15 movies. But you can choose to buy them wherever you please! *(I would love to collect some of the Classics for her! Walmart has Bambi and Dumbo!)* I am also requesting they are Child-Friendly, animated—not neccesarily Disney, but idealy, yes, Haha! :)

HERE IS THE LIST OF MOVIES SHE HAS ALREADY!
James and the Giant Peach
Wall-E
Ratatouille
The Lion King
Alice in Wonderland
And she will be getting Finding Nemo from an unnamed family
    member :)

It would mean alot to us if she got at least **ONE** movie from everyone. It would be much easier to travel with, but if you happen to get her something else that is also fine. You do not have to tell me what movie you are getting for her!! But I would love to know who will be interested in getting her a movie. Gift Cards are also acceptable.

Thank you everyone! Avery is going to have a great xmas home with her whole family no matter what she gets! :)

PS: YOU ARE NOT OBLIGED YOU GET HER A MOVIE! I just thought it would be a great, small, cheap gift and travel friendly! :) Thank you!

Friends, Family, Acquaintances, and Countrymen,

This year we're asking everyone in the greater metropolitan area to please purchase at least ONE Disney movie for our young daughter for Xmas. We are hoping to build her a HUGE collection so that she owns every animated movie ever made. Classics are preferred, but the primary goal is for her to just own a shitload of movies. We're relying on your help to make it happen, **BUT PLEASE DO NOT FEEL OBLIGATED.** *:)*

15

Inappropriate Parenting

When you're in the habit of relaying your day-to-day life to friends and followers, the chances of saying something dumb online increase considerably. But what amuse me are the updates written by people who see nothing wrong with typing exactly what's on their mind, even if what they write paints them as being potentially bad at parenting. That's not to say that I'm judging whether people should be responsible for caring for their children so much as I'm judging their decision to post certain pieces of information on social media.

In fact, in some ways sharing embarrassing or questionable information about yourself or your parenting style online is *worse*, because you can't really redeem yourself after the fact. It's not like being at a party and asking, "Who needs a babysitter when you've got *Dora the Explorer*, am I right?" and quickly seeing by the looks on people's faces that what you just said was stupid. On the Internet, when you say something like that, you have no way of knowing how it's interpreted unless someone leaves a comment. And yet despite that potential for confusion, people say the first thing that pops into their mind all the time. Sure, it's usually harmless, and the Internet moves at such a fast pace that their friends will probably forget it within seconds, but it's still a risk that I don't recommend taking. Unless of course you don't mind looking totally foolish, in which case, carry on! There's nothing more enjoyable than reading about other people's stupidity online.

 Kimberly So my daughter is sitting on the potty . . . grabs a tampon . . . and sticks it between her legs . . . how in the world does she know where that goes??!!!???
2 minutes ago • Like • Comment

> **Erin** TMI, TMI, TMI . . . take that off, OMG. Cute, but too personal!
> 1 minute ago • Like

Erin is having an almost visceral reaction to Kimberly's status update. As a woman, you're either the type to tell everyone under the sun that you've got your period or you're the type to keep the information to yourself and suffer in silence. I'm guessing Kimberly is the former, and therefore sees nothing wrong with making a joke about her toddler daughter attempting to insert a tampon between her legs—something that would make most women (and men!) squirm. It's one thing to notice your kid playing around with tampons in the bathroom, but it's another thing to post about it on Facebook.

Chelsea is holding an open house for potential paternity test candidates. I have to narrow this list down and figure out who my daughter's father is. It should be located at 218 Meadow Street from 6–8 on Sunday. If you slept with me in March of 2012, please show up for your free swab! This is faster than trying to cross you guys off my list one by one.

Tuesday at 3:27pm • Like • Comment

I'm assuming Chelsea is posting this exact message on Facebook, Craigslist, MySpace, Twitter, Bebo . . . I mean this gent could be anywhere. Let's not forget that Chelsea slept with *a lot* of guys in March of '12 aka "March Madness." Some bets were made, a few strip poker games were lost . . . you know how it goes.

 Josh Real Question: People with daughters, Can you live with the fact that 1 day, Someone will bust one in your lil' girl's face? Its killing me!!!

3 hours ago via mobile • Like • Comment

> **Chad** Oooh weeee, I don't want a daughter no more thanks to dat question dammit!!! Lol
>
> 3 hours ago • Like

> **Brandi** Wow. Just wow.
>
> 3 hours ago • Like

Sometimes I look at guys like Josh and wonder, "What are they really thinking?" Is the seemingly dim exterior of a certain type of dude actually just a façade for hyper-intelligence? If I see Josh, let's say, eating a double serving of nachos at a baseball game while wearing a Hooters shirt, why should I assume he's not contemplating a series of advanced mathematical formulas to help fix the crippling economic crisis? Maybe he is!

Or, judging by this status update, maybe he's just pondering the day his little girl will receive her first money shot. You never really know what's going on in people's heads.

 Jenna Just a tid bit for anyone who is pregnant to chew on . . . If you dye your hair during pregnancy your child can be born with whatever color you dyed your hair . . . interesting and worth knowing.
4 hours ago • Like • Comment

> **Jasmine** That is a freaking myth. Lol. I dyed my hair when i was pregnant and Lily doesn't have that hair color. Lol. If that were true she would have bleach blonde and fire red high lights!! :p of course that would be freaking cute, but she doesnt . . . she has my natural hair color . . . so yeah . . . i say that is a myth.
> 4 hours ago • Like

> **Jenna** just wait she could have little high lights when she gets more hair . . . you never know . . . myth or not tho I'm not gonna tempt fate . . . i want Jazzlyn to have my red hair so bad . . .
> 4 hours ago • Like

This is like when you're standing in line for a ride at an amusement park and you overhear two people having the *dumbest* conversation you've ever heard for twenty-five minutes straight. And it's so nonsensical that you can't even properly recap it later, except to say that it was amazing.

I would never be able to do justice to the greatness of this conversation by attempting to retell it to a friend, but suffice to say I'm both shocked and impressed with Jenna's willingness to expose her inanity in such a public forum. I'm usually way too nervous to admit that I haven't heard of a certain band, so for her to just put herself out there like that is impressive.

16
Loss of Identity

I f there's one thing people can do that will change their lives forever, it's having a baby. And never is this fact more evident than on social media sites. For most parents, making a production out of this new life development is not only natural, it's expected. It's a wonderful time full of new experiences and cherished memories.

That is, until a parent becomes so obsessed with her baby that she forgets what it was like when she *didn't* have a baby. What did she talk about? How could anything be worth discussing that's more interesting than the gassy smile of a newborn? For some parents, this question looms large, and the person they used to be starts to slowly disappear. Status updates go from a picture of a glass of wine with the caption "Time to unwind!" to pictures of their baby sleeping with the caption "Day 19. The little stinker fell asleep after a giant blowout!"

Their friends grit their teeth and think, "This won't last forever. I haven't lost my friend forever!" They reminisce momentarily about being roommates in college or consoling each other after breakups, just before reading farther down their newsfeeds another update that says, "Jeremiah farted during dinner tonight and sounded just like his Daddy!" And with that, the new parents' friends begin to mourn the loss of a friendship that once withstood a months-long fight over the cable bill.

Kelsey Should put 'Harper' in my hobbies/interests and erase everything else haha
3 hours ago • Like • Comment

This would be funny if "Harper" was a pet name for Kelsey's new Tamagotchi, but since it's the name of her actual baby, it's more like "Haha, I'm just a puddle of mom now." If you catch yourself making a joke that you should erase your former interests and replace them with your child, you're about two weeks away from calling sweatpants your "mom uniform."

Dorothy I am sitting here trying to figure out what to put as a status that doesn't talk about Aubrey . . . Im at a loss.
4 hours ago • Like • Comment

> **Stephanie** That is your future too! May be annoying to people who aren't parents . . . but those of us who are are right there with you!
> 5 minutes ago • Like

I'm imagining Dorothy painfully attempting to craft a status update on her computer while having an inner dialogue.

"So today Aubrey and I . . ." No, wait. Hmm. Okay, got it. "Earlier today at the farmer's market, Aubrey ate some blueberries and . . ." Oh, whoops! That didn't work, either, darn it. Oh, but wait, the trip to Target where I got new bras! I'll post about that. "Just got some new bras at Target after taking a nice sweet nap with Aubrey." Good enough!

About Kirsten I'm fun. Deal with it. I'm a hardcore Mommy, if you aren't prepared to hear all about my precious children, don't talk to me! ;)

Employers **CEO of My Home** Yep . . . I totally run this house! With some help from my wonderful hubby. I love (almost) every minute of staying home with my kids and wouldn't trade it for anything!

Kirsten I have decided that stay at home moms are also grossly underpaid. I am starting a union. "Fair wages, more sleep! Fair wages, more sleep!" Who's with me? ;)
46 minutes ago • Like • Comment
👍 **4 people** like this.

Kirsten My children are awful today!!!!
Friday at 10:42am • Like • Comment

Kirsten I don't get sick days. I don't get to call off and sleep in. I am EXHAUSTED! Caty has had me up the last two nights and I am about to be beyond functioning.
Wednesday at 4:56pm • Like • Comment

Kirsten I'm kind of tired of society.
Wednesday at 11:01am • Like • Comment

This whole submission sounds like a spiral into Isolationville. And I'm easily able to imagine the book-turned-movie *Stay-at-Home Mom: When Love Turns to Anger*. In a way, this is what makes social media so entertaining. Watching people "change" over time—through personal breakups, career transitions, weight fluctuations, etc.—can feel like your own little reality television show starring everyone you've ever known. But at some point that entertainment becomes voyeuristic awkwardness, particularly when a person who claims to love (almost) every minute of her life starts condemning society. This is one of those times.

Anne Mothers, for the love of all things good, please stop calling yourselves "Mommy" as if it's a first person pronoun. It's not.
about an hour ago • Like • Comment

> **Melissa** Then what should we call ourselves?? Last time I checked my name has been Mommy since 3/29/10 and that's what I respond to, and that's how I refer to myself to my kids so they know my name. :)
> 40 minutes ago • Like

> **Samantha** Indeed, the mommies can try using "I" sometimes.
> 9 minutes ago • Like

There isn't a logical defense to calling yourself Mommy around grown adults. It just shouldn't be done. If you can't remember a good reason to refer to yourself by your first name, you've got problems. Make little sticky reminders that say, "My name is Melissa" and put them around the house if you have to, but don't lose your identity just because you've had children.

17

Mama Drama

Daytime television has always been an entertaining mud pit of talk-show drama, but these days, if you want to catch some real drama, you have to tune into Facebook. For one thing, the arguments that play out in the social media sphere are totally legit. No one is paying people to pretend to insult each other and call each other out in a public forum. No one is handing anyone a script and saying, "Action!" before the crazy hits the fan. On social networking sites, the drama is not only real, but it plays out in real time. It's like watching people fight from the comfort of your couch without ordering anything off of pay-per-view. In short, it is one of the greatest outcomes of parent overshare on social media that I've come across.

I'm not saying that people *should* engage in public arguments on Facebook, but let's be honest, watching other people have silly disputes is a much-beloved pastime for a certain generation. I'd even go so far as to say that the "Jerry Springer generation" is probably more inclined to openly argue on social media, and many of the people who fit that description are now young parents. So it makes sense that Facebook is now being used as a virtual boxing ring for parents who have some words they'd like to get off their chest, be it with a group, a business, or a friend. And watching the drama "unfold" in the form of comments and status updates couldn't be more intoxicating. In a sea of dirty diapers and stories about projectile puke, it's nice to see people getting back to basics. Screw the etiquette! Long live the mama drama!

 Kristina EVERYONE THAT'S WOORIED ABOUT WHICH ONE OF MY DAUGHTERS IS **PREGNANT** MIND YOUR BIZZ. EVERYONE IS GROWN, THEY R OLD ENOUGH TO HAVE A KID IF THEY WANT. MOST OF YALL HAD A KID AT 15 SO HOW CAN U TALK ABOUT THEM. BY THE WAY YALL TALKING BOUT THE WRONG DAUGHTER LMAO SMFH!!!! SOME PPL NEED TO GET A LIFE
22 minutes ago via mobile • Like • Comment

This is some mama drama FOR REAL. Multiple mamas, multiple dramas, and there's even a curveball thrown in the mix since everyone is apparently talking about the wrong daughter. People should stop "woorying" about which of Kristina's teenaged daughters is pregnant and mind their bizz!

 Kara sorry guys but i won't be at my baby shower i have appt i have to be at but jeff and kyle will still be there
Yesterday at 8:03pm • Like • Comment

> **Jackie** Appointment?? i heard u were in jail.
> Yesterday at 8:18pm • Like

Derrick that is because you are in jail but hang tight we will figure something out

16 hours ago • Like

Kara Sorry, was trying to keep kara's personal information off of Facebook. I think she would have preferred it that way; but if you would rather tell the whole world and all her friends I can't stop you.

7 hours ago • Like

Question: Is it mama drama if only one mama has drama? Answer: Yes, if said drama involves jail time.

 Alana thanks to those of you that thought to call dante today im dissappointed that a few select people didnt even bother to call him today not that it bothers him but it's the point

13 minutes ago • Like • Comment

> **Alana** oh and thanks to those of you that sent him wishes on here too
>
> 12 minutes ago • Like
>
> **Justin** tell him i said happy birthay
>
> 6 minutes ago • Like
>
> **Alana** i will thaks justin . . . . . the people that this message is meant for will know who they are when they read it SO IF YOU THINK THIS IS ABOUT YOU THEN YOU ARE PROBABLY RIGHT
>
> 2 minutes ago • Like

The people who this message is for sure are going to be SORRY when they catch up on their Facebook newsfeeds! Not that the baby is bothered, per se, but that's not the point. The point is that an innocent child deserved a birthday phone call, which a few people didn't provide, and now those people are going to be shamed. They knew better than to disappoint a little baby and his mother like that, but they went right ahead and did it anyway.

Miranda Amelia is selling Girl Scout cookies this year so if u want some let me know
16 hours ago • Like • Comment

> **Sally** I am a g.s. leader and in our annual cookie meeting with the council, parents are spose to be banned from advertising this on Facebook because of a big conflict last year since it's the parent selling and not the girl. If this is sent in to your area council, her troop will loose all their profit.
> 15 hours ago • Like

> **Elena** Actually from what I understand it can be posted on Facebook for parents to let other family members know. It just can't be posted for a website or other use in order to sell to people not personally known.
> 15 hours ago • Like

> **Sally** OK, I'll send the sheet and while I am at it, I am printing this to send into the council so now her troop will see no profit. The only terms you can use is "it's cookie time."
> 15 hours ago • Like

> **Elena** Wow. Actually I have the information sheet in front of me from my daughter's Girl Scout troop and it clearly states "Girls may use e-mail and age appropriate online social networking sites to inform customers about cookie sales, however direct internet sales are not allowed." I believe Miranda is following

those guidelines. She informed customers that the sales are going on. She didn't conduct a sale online nor did she solicit customers. If you're a Girl Scout leader or a Girl Scout mother I feel sad for the people you're affiliated with. Not the Girl Scout persona that should be representing Girl Scouts.

15 hours ago • Like

👍 **1 person** likes this

Felicia Geeze no wonder I don't buy Girl Scout cookies . . .

14 hours ago • Like

It's cookie time, bitches. And by "cookie time" I mean the annual "Girl Scouts Cookie Season *SHOWDOWN!!!*" Trust me, *you don't wanna fuck with troop leaders.* Those ladies have an appetite for destruction.

18

Mom Sex Talk

y mother always told me that certain things should remain a mystery. Details about pregnancy, birth, and basic hygiene are best kept secret, perhaps not from a person's partner or close friends, but certainly from former coworkers, bosses, professors, and mothers-in-law. I don't typically consider myself a prude, but I'm also not going to reveal every aspect of my body, health, and sex life to the entire world via status updates. Why would I want the whole world to know that I hate shaving my legs, or that I'd rather eat moldy vegetables than wash my hair? Why would I joke about my sex life in a public forum when people are already busy enough with their own? And why, oh WHY, would I share details about my vagina with hundreds of Facebook friends and Twitter followers if everyone already knows it's suffered the wrath of a several-pound baby? (It hasn't, by the way. *Yet*. *shudder*)

But what is it about having a baby that suddenly increases the amount of oversharing done by women online? I can't imagine being so comfortable with my body or so free with my sex life that I want to share those things with my fifth-grade lab partner as he eats a turkey sub and scrolls through his newsfeed on a Tuesday afternoon. But despite my reservations, it appears many other women feel the opposite. They share in the notion that our bodies are natural and nature is beautiful and babies are gifts and blah blah blah, let's talk about it!

 Rhonda Well my belly has gotten so big that I haven't seen my kitty kat in months . . . so, my old man trimmed the hedges for me ;) #goodman

16 hours ago • Like • Comment

👍 **13 people** like this.

> **Gabe** Wow
>
> 16 hours ago • Like
>
> ---
>
> **Rhonda** lol
>
> 15 hours ago • Like
>
> ---
>
> **Meadow** THX FOR SHARING!!! WOW!!! T.M.I.!!!
>
> 15 hours ago • Like
>
> ---
>
> **Claudia** THATS SO HE CAN FIND IT. LMAO. HE'S LIKE LAY DOWN SO I CAN GIVE U A CREW CUT. LMFAO!!!!
>
> 14 hours ago • Like
>
> ---
>
> **Elliot** I wondered why it was so quiet up there for SO LONG! (ROTFL)
>
> 10 hours ago • Like
>
> ---
>
> **Elliot** I see you 'forgot' to mention that you are one centimeter dilated!!! :-)
>
> 10 hours ago • Like

Gabe Ummmmmmm eeew much?! ;-)

9 hours ago • Like

Dimitri lololol

8 hours ago • Like

Without fail, every time someone says "LMFAO" or "ROTFL" on social media, it's the opposite of such a thing. I am now picturing Rhonda's giant bush getting trimmed with a weedwacker and a pair of hedge shears.

 Kim NSFR = Not Safe for Relatives! I just heard an all-too-familiar sound coming out of the bathroom. I walk in to find my son standing over the toilet with my rabbit pearl. "Do you know what that is?" I ask as calmly as possible. "A PENIS!" he replied, proudly. Indeed. Is there enough therapy in the world that will make Mama preferring them 9 inches, with a spinning head, in a shade of pretty pink, okay?

about an hour ago • Like • Comment

> **Annie** OH . . . MY . . . GOD . . . yeah . . . I had to spell that out! lol Too freakin funny! You need a better hiding place!
>
> 54 minutes ago • Like

> **Annie** I put mine in purses hanging in my closet, not being used. The other night I had a dream that I let a friend borrow a purse and totally forgot to take "my friend" out of it!! Hahaha! Guess I need a new hiding place too . . . huh?
>
> 53 minutes ago • Like

Whoa, whoa, whoa. Say what?! Kim's son found her vibrator—which, hey, nothing wrong with a lady who likes to be satisfied—and

then held it over the toilet as he would his own "little buddy"—
which, hey, you know how kids are—and then she wrote about it
online? That's the part that trips me up. Am I the only person who
wouldn't want her digital network to read about her nine-inch,
spinning-head vibrator preferences on the Internet?

Tamara Can we say sexual frustration! I really hate this post-
pregnancy stuff. I just want to get back to our norm and have the
desire to get there. :/
10:12pm • Like • Comment
👍 **2 people** like this.

> **Jessie** You don't bother me! I hear ya girl! It'll be over soon!
> 12:55am • Like

> **Elizabeth** a lot of people relate, we just don't talk about it on FB,
> now Wed. morning Bible study? that's a different thing :)
> 7:17am • Like

Ah, the things that get discussed during Bible study (or it's drag
queen sister, Bible studay). Talk about raunchy! That's what Bible
study is for! Why overshare on a massively public scale when you
could just share those private bits of information among a select
group of practicing Christians while in the presence of God?

Hailey House is cleaned . . . the kids are napping . . . maybe i'll
wash my cootch and put on something sexy just because ♥
5:16pm • Like • Comment
👍 **2 people** like this.

> **Morgan** TMI . . . . . hahahah
> 5:57pm • Like

Mary Lol, the Joy! It's nice to feel clean & sexy after ALL is said & done, kid's, housework etc..

6:12pm • Like

Julieanne Um. Wow.

7:02pm • Like

Rachael Your honesty is hilarious!

7:08pm • Like 👍 1 person

Chip TMI, Dear.

5:14pm • Like

Suzie It does make you feel better from time to time. Pour a cheap glass of wine and put in a dirty movie. You'll feel like a whole new woman.

8:19am • Like

I can't tell you how many times I've said to my girlfriends, "Ladies, do you know what we all need to do tonight? We need to slip on a little lingerie, wash our old cootches, and put on a dirty movie. We deserve it."

19

Momedy

There's a certain brand of mom humor—much like there are certain brands of mom jeans—and it's a little hard to describe. Mom comedy, or "momedy," ranges from genuinely funny to stab-you-in-the-eye cringe-worthy humor, but the one thing every type of momedy status update has in common is that the joke ultimately only appeals to parents.

If a parenting "joke" makes you awkwardly laugh, reflexively look away, or feel like punching a wall, that's how you know it's momedy.

Interestingly, momedy is much more prevalent on social media than it is in real life. In real life, most parents don't communicate every little thing they find hilarious about their children because they know that it's probably "a mom thing." On sites like Facebook, however, momedy is pervasive. The potential for using the site as both a baby book and a stage for open-mic-night-style comedy is simply too irresistible to pass up. Jokes range from "kids say the darndest things" to "poop shaped like animals." Momedy is the joke equivalent of having a face that only a mother could love.

 Karyn How many stay-at-home moms does it take to change a lightbulb? HA! Just me; there's nobody around to help! Off on lightbulb duty . . .

1 hour ago via mobile • Like • Comment

👍 **2 people** like this.

Oh, Karyn. How I wish you hadn't just made that joke. Not only was it not funny, but in the time it took you to make it, you could've changed that lightbulb. *Twice.* It takes less time to change a lightbulb than it takes to eat a grape.

Lorena I swear I need to write a book of Abigail's quips. Today I found her sitting on the toilet eatting a Pop-Tart. She explains she is doing so because they give her diarrhea so she is just waiting for it to occur.

about an hour ago • Like • Comment

👍 Cate and 13 others like this.

> **Lorena** I told her too if they make her sick, not to eat them but she exclaimed they are sooooo good! lol
>
> about an hour ago • Like
>
> **Heather** Holy Sh$$ that girl is hilarious! Yes, you do need to start writing these down!
>
> about an hour ago • Like 👍 2 people
>
> **Megan** Lmao! I agree, I would start writing
>
> about an hour ago • Like
>
> **Veronica** Haha that's great!
>
> about an hour ago • Like
>
> **Alex** thats genius!
>
> about an hour ago • Like
>
> **Debra** so funny. she is a cutie.
>
> about an hour ago • Like

Start writing, Lorena!!! START. WRITING. These little nuggets (no pun intended! Haha!) are comedy gold. At the very least, start a blog called *Abigail Says*. That little girl is too dang precious for words, and I haven't heard an absolutely *hysterical* joke about Pop-Tarts giving a person diarrhea in a *long* time. She's legendary!

Candice Mason just coined the smell of his poop as "a bucket of dead fish and old food with a nacho in the middle." LMMFAO!!!!!!!!!!!!!!!!!!!!! I might actually die from how funny that is. Then he just remarked, "Dad says it smells like dead bats in a cave"!!!!! I seriously may not survive the night. Ow.

19 minutes ago • Like • Comment

👍 **Sarah and 3 others** like this.

> **Candice** Apparently, if you don't AGREE with Mason, "then you don't have a MIIIIIIND!!!!!!" Ha ha ha ha!
>
> 14 minutes ago • Like

> **Candice** P.S. If you're offended by posts about what my kid's poop smells like, you either a) don't really KNOW me or b) should seriously consider un-friending me, 'cause it's probably just gonna happen again next week.
>
> 10 minutes ago • Like

> **Tess** What are you feeding him???
>
> 8 minutes ago • Like 👍 1 person

> **Candice** Dead fish and nachos . . . duh! LMAO!
>
> 7 minutes ago • Like 👍 1 person

> **Candice** Honestly, if my kid were any funnier, I would be FINED.
>
> 3 minutes ago • Like

Honestly, if I got stuck in an elevator with Candice for an hour, I would be FINED! Because there is no way I would make it out of there without metaphorically filling a life-sized swear jar. I almost feel like this thread has put me into a state of hypnotic anger. Each comment takes me deeper and deeper into a state of "ZOMG this chick fucking sucks."

Tina So, Maya's sitting on her potty, and says, "Mommy, I'm peeing so my poop has something to swim in!"

58 minutes ago • Like • Comment

👍 **3 people** like this.

> **Nancy** Lmao that is so cute
>
> 7 minutes ago • Like

Haha, look at that, Maya's poop can do the backstroke! Look, now it's doing the butterfly! Now two poops are competing in a swim meet, how funny is that? Lmao, kids are so cute.

20

Mommyjacking

A simple word can have a complex meaning, and that's where our story begins with mommyjacking. "Mommyjacking" is defined as a parent hijacking a friend's status update to talk about parenting—but oh, it's so much more than that. It's the self-involved, yet extremely common, parental habit of injecting tidbits about one's children into conversations in a way that wasn't really possible before social media existed.

Having a bad day at work? Mommyjacked. Just got engaged? Mommyjacked. Family pet passed away? You guessed it. That shit's gonna get MJed. No status is safe, because mommyjackers don't see obstacles; they see opportunity. They love a challenge. And they're willing to put up a fight to get the word out that today is little Braedyn's eleven-and-a-half-week birthday, and *yes*, he has a registry.

JoAnn "Don't say you don't have enough time. You have exactly the same number of hours per day that were given to Helen Keller, Pasteur, Michaelangelo, Mother Teresa, Leonardo da Vinci, Thomas Jefferson, and Albert Einstein."—H. Jackson Brown

2 hours ago • Like • Comment

👍 **Dionne** likes this.

> **Ashley** amen! Although, I don't think any of these ladies had kids, and you know the men even if they had kids didn't have any parental responsibilities for the most part.
>
> about an hour ago • Like

I'm not saying Mother Teresa and Helen Keller weren't truly stupendous people. Life-changers, even. What with Mother Teresa's whole ministry to the sick and poor and Helen Keller's overcoming adversity as a deaf-blind person. I mean, sure. Looks great on paper. But let me ask you just one little question that you may not have considered: Were these women mothers?

 Holly went from being "in a relationship" to "single."

16 hours ago • Like • Comment

> **Daisy** :(Dislike
>
> 16 hours ago • Like

> **Leigh** Hey love when do u work? Id love to show u my Liam! He deff will cheer u up :)
>
> 13 hours ago • Like

Unless "Liam" is a code word for a magnum-sized bottle of wine and a pint of ice cream, I'm guessing Holly won't feel too perked up by Leigh's offer, but hey, you never know. Sometimes the best way to feel better after a breakup is by meeting your friend's adorable baby. Wait . . . no, it isn't.

Nichole Today has to be the worst day of the year so far. Everything that could go wrong did go wrong.

14 hours ago • Like • Comment

> **Martene** i'm so sorry. it will get better.
>
> 12 hours ago • Like

> **Vanessa** I'm sorry. :/
>
> 11 hours ago • Like

> **Ginny** Guess what went right? Ava is 6 today! We love you.
>
> 10 hours ago • Like

"Sorry you're depressed and having a bad day, but, um . . . MY LITTLE GIRL TURNED 6 TODAY! *BOOM IN YO FACE!!!!!*"

Sabrina I can't believe that I am getting married in a month! Woohoo!

10 minutes ago • Like • Comment

👍 **2 people** like this.

> **Todd** Time flies! Wow. My daughter will be 3 next month and my son 1 three days later.
>
> 8 minutes ago • Like

Hoo-boy! Time, she's tricky. Sabrina is getting married in a month, and Todd's kids are—believe it or not—both having birthdays. Which has nothing to do with Sabrina, per se, but hey, who cares? When Todd hears "next month" he thinks, "my kids' birthdays," so why shouldn't he share the information? It's a celebration! On Sabrina's wall. For his kids. And for Sabrina, too . . . sort of!

 Mommyjacking Variations

The diverse selection of mommyjackings I've encountered makes me feel like a cultural anthropologist who's onto something "big." I've discovered categories, and subcategories, and I've often wondered if it's even possible for there to be a subject that cannot be mommyjacked. So far in my vast studies, it doesn't appear that there is.

THE PETJACKER

Your pet may be sweet, cute, and loyal, but it will never be a baby.

Gabrielle There is nothing better than to come home to 3 dogs who act like the best moment of their lives was the moment you walked through that door.

10 hours ago • Like • Comment

👍 **7 people** like this.

> **Mark** Yay
> 10 hours ago • Like

> **David** Just wait til you have kids !
> 3 hours ago • Like

THE SCHOOLJACKER

Your academic achievements are a justifiable point of pride, but school is merely a stepping-stone to the most important achievement of all: parenthood.

Danica I passed my dissertation defense! I'm a doctor! I have a lot of revisions to make to my dissertation but other than that I'm doing pretty great!

17 hours ago • Like • Comment

👍 **51 people** like this.

> **Shelley** Congratulations!
>
> 17 hours ago • Like
>
> **Evan** Congratulations!
>
> 17 hours ago • Like
>
> **Ruth** Congratulations!!! That's fantastic!
>
> 16 hours ago • Like
>
> **Darcy** Congratulations Doctor!!
>
> 16 hours ago • Like
>
> **Camille** Yippee. How exciting. Now you need the title of "mommy." Sorry, I just know what an amazing mom you'll be. Can't wait to see you guys at Rachel's wedding. Congrats.
>
> 15 hours ago • Like

THE DEATHJACKER

The world does not stop spinning just because you've suffered the loss of a loved one. In fact, babies are being born and children are getting older by the minute! Isn't life grand?

Doree Tomorrow would have been my brother-in-law Mike's 60th birthday. Not a day goes by that I don't think about him. Gone too soon and still loved so much. Nick and I are taking care of your Ma, Mike . . . I know you can see that. RIP. I love you forever and miss you beyond words!

2 hours ago • Like • Comment

👍 **5 people** like this.

Bevin Austin will be 8 tomorrow :)

2 hours ago • Like

THE NON-SEQUITURJACKER

The non-sequiturjacker pays no mind to what you're saying *and* makes no sense, so don't try to figure out what the random comments mean. Just go with it.

Jolene Monday Monday, Can't trust that day, Monday Monday, Sometimes it just turns out that way

34 minutes ago • Like • Comment

Vicki Kaitlin said mamma

31 minutes ago • Like

21

Mompetitions

arl Jung once said, "Nothing has a stronger influence psy-chologically on their environment and especially on their children than the unlived life of the parent." Never has this quote been truer or more evident than in today's parenting culture. Parent competitions, also lovingly known as mompetitions, exist both in real life and online, and they're defined by obnoxious sports-like one-upping by people who think their methods of parenting are far superior to those of their friends and that their children are the most gifted. The definition of "gifted" can range from a baby who can roll over to a four-year-old whose parents insist that he knows all of the presidents in chronological order and can speak fluent Mandarin while balancing on his head.

The beauty of witnessing a mompetition on the Internet is that it's one of the rare times people catch a glimpse of just how far off the deep end their friend has gone since having a baby. It's one thing to read a status update about a friend's preferred parenting methods, but it's another to watch her rail on others for parenting differently. Breastfeeding is a good example of this, because the debate over breastfeeding vs. formula is a never-ending judgment-fest of insensitivity and condescension. For some reason, women (and men!) who compete in mompetitions enjoy this type of verbal sparring. It's like a hazing ritual for yuppies who only want the best for their children. Don't even think about entering the ring if you're not prepared to take it all the way. You can't start at comparing weight percentiles and then stop at peanut allergies. It just doesn't work like that.

Elissa Two jobs and an almost two year old = zombie Elissa. x_x
about an hour ago • Like • Comment
👍 **Kelly** likes this.

> **Gia** 3 jobs and an almost 7 month old . . .
> 57 minutes ago • Like

Technically this exchange could go on forever, with more people jumping in on the mixing 'n' matching to determine precisely who's got it the worst. What's more debilitating: One job with three kids, two jobs with two kids, or three jobs with a four-month-old and a parakeet?

Kristy My daughter brought all of her grades up this semester. I am so proud of her!!
about an hour ago • Like • Comment
👍 **5 people** like this.

Andrea Nice going! My son made the honor roll for the second time in a row :)

21 minutes ago • Like

Aw, your kid brought her grades up? That's cute. My child made the honor roll so we're EXTRA proud of her achievements. :) Not that a child bringing her grades up isn't a huge feat. It totally is! But nothing is better than honor roll.

 Carolyn Lucy took 2 steps today!! 9 months old and already trying to walk! :D

2 hours ago • Like • Comment

👍 **Sarah and 13 others** like this.

> **Kevin** AWESOME!
>
> 2 hours ago • Like

> **Mona** YAYYYYYYYYYYYYY GO LUCYYYY—sooo cute!
>
> 2 hours ago • Like

> **Amy** Carter walked at 9 months, Lillien at 8.
>
> 2 hours ago • Like

Amy's point is pretty easy to decipher: Whatever Lucy does, it will never compete with Carter or Lillien. *Ever.* If Lucy starts talking at twelve months, Carolyn will quickly learn that Amy's kids started talking at twelve *weeks.* If Lucy starts kindergarten a year early, Carolyn will receive a singing telegram informing her that Amy's kids started school in utero. By the time Lucy graduates from high school, there will be bronze statues erected in the town square of Carter and

Lillien listing all of their accomplishments, including all of the charity work they've done and how many Facebook friends they have. When you're the best, you *act like* you're the best.

Jane Women who can cope with the terrible twos can cope with anything

4 hours ago • Like • Comment

👍 **Dani, Michele and 7 others** like this.

Darlene wait until he is 3 . . . . . .

4 hours ago • Like

Lesley yeah I had no problem with the two but boy my little one is 3 now and boy I wish she was two again!!!

4 hours ago • Like

Becki yeah i agree three is worse

4 hours ago • Like

Ellie That is for sure

4 hours ago • Like

Ann-Marie i will trade you your two year old for my two eight year olds

4 hours ago • Like

Ellie meh my 6 yr old was good at 2 but bad at 3 . . . but my 2 yr old now is way worse then my 6 yr old was so i'm thinking maybe some go through terrible 2s and some terrible 3s

4 hours ago • Like

Eryka it's just a leadup and training session for teenage years!

4 hours ago • Like

Ha! Jane thinks two is bad? *Dream on, Jane.* Why not try age three? Or age four with an allergy to all foods containing protein?! Or try twins, how about that?! Did Jane ever think of people who have twins? She mentions the terrible twos, but try experiencing the terrible twos with terrible twins! Jane thinks she can survive anything just because she's lived through a child's first twenty-four months? Now that's rich! Good thing she has some awesome friends to set her straight! Just wait until that two-year-old is a teenager!

22

My Kid Is Awesome

In today's excellence-driven kid culture, it goes without saying that parents like to brag about their offspring on social media. Unlike some of the more questionable and disgusting things parents post, these braggart updates tend to exist in more of a gray area. Parents have been bragging about their kids since the beginning of time (or at least in recent centuries), and technically there's nothing wrong with parents giving shout-outs to their kids for their achievements (unless they're competing in mompetitions about weight percentiles).

The problem is that many of the braggart status updates parents write seem to be more about patting *themselves* on the back than their kids (whose backs I presume they pat at home, away from the computer). And while that's all well and good, because I understand that it's just in some people's DNA to grandstand, this sharing tendency comes off as obnoxious at best and deluded at worst. Yes, everybody thinks it's fucking awesome that your son has learned how to wave hello and your daughter got an A on her report on crustaceans, but not so awesome that they want to read about it daily. Honestly, people are perfectly fine with just knowing that your kid is vaccinated, happy, and educated. No other details needed.

 Hilary Brooklyn's vocabulary

Duck

123456

Juice

Sit

Fruit

Head

Sholders

Knees

Toes

Eyes

Ear

Mouth

Nose

Teeth

Tounge

Hand

Finger

Feet

Phone

Stairs.

. . .

My boy is fuggggin smart

March 13 at 9:27pm via mobile • Like • Comment

One thing is certain: This family sings a lot of "Head, Shoulders, Knees, and Toes."

Aileen I hate it when people compare their kid to Elijah and then say crap like "Why can't you be that smart?" It makes me feel like my son is a freak or something.

11 hours ago • Like • Comment

> **Lily** geez, nice parents. Elijah isn't a freak, he just has intelligent parents, so it's in his genes lol
>
> 10 hours ago • Like

> **Aileen** It's not just one family, it's every single time we take him in public, since he was like 10 months. It's annoying, and I wish people would keep their mouths shut. The boy's already arrogant, he doesn't need a bigger ego!
>
> 10 hours ago • Like

> **Grace** I get that a lot with Drew too. It makes me feel so awkward.
>
> 14 minutes ago • Like

> **Victoria** My kids are the same way. Landon used to try and talk to other boys when he was 18 months old and at first they thought "Who is this baby?" but because he understood and was so articulate, they eventually warmed up to him and allowed him to play. Sophia is going through the same thing, she uses her words and understands more than most other 3 year olds. She hardly has any friends her age because of it.
>
> 14 minutes ago • Like

Here we have to take the parents at their word that their kids are "freakishly" smart. No specific examples are cited to prove their kids' intelligence, but I am *majorly* feeling the emotional severity of Aileen, Grace, and Victoria's comments. Therefore, their kids MUST be smart! Otherwise why would they be so tormented by all the incessant praise? It's clear that because Elijah, Drew, and Sophia are so smart, they have massive egos and no friends. That's just what happens when you're born into the world with good genes. It's a blessing, but, boy, is it tough to be marginalized.

Audrey My 2 year old likes to flip through his Dad's Economist magazine, trying to buy books for "his age group" is laughable.
16 hours ago • Like • Comment

> **Natasha** That kid is smart
> 14 hours ago • Like

Audrey is one proud mom. Her kid is so smart, he knows how to flip through the pages of a magazine. And not just any old magazine, but the *Economist* magazine. It sure can be hard to find books for a kid who's leaps and bounds away from "his age group" in reading comprehension. It's laughable, actually. Totally fucking hilarious. Like Audrey is holding her stomach from laughing so hard at the mere thought of handing her child a book for two-year-olds. *The Very Hungry Caterpillar*? Okay, now that is just FUNNY.

Marilyn Gave Oliver a spinach salad for dinner . . . he wouldn't eat it until I wilted the spinach with garlic and lemon zest . . . I shall never underestimate his profound palate
51 minutes ago • Like • Comment

> **Robert** You mean he likes food that's edible?
> 52 minutes ago • Like

Liz Chef in the making?!?!
5 minutes ago • Like

I have to give it to Robert for his comment, which is a thing of beauty, because honestly, who the hell just eats spinach raw and acts like it tastes good? Certainly not an eighteen-month-old, which is the age of the child in this example. You know—the child who wouldn't eat spinach for dinner until it was "wilted with garlic and lemon zest"? Something tells me he would've been even happier with it covered in applesauce.

23
Oversharing in Public

If there's one subject that irritates me more than any other, it's parents who act like assholes in public. Whether it's in a restaurant, a museum, some mode of transportation, or even just a public bathroom, I believe that the modicum of decorum that used to exist among parents has all but disappeared.

I don't know when life with kids became so much of a struggle. When I asked my own mother if she ever washed my diarrhea-covered ass off in a public restroom sink, she choked on her sweet tea. When I asked my father if he ever considered "retaliating" against an airline that didn't provide changing tables by changing me on the seat, he said, "I think we would have figured out an alternative," like I'd just asked him to put on a clown suit covered in baby crap. Today's parents, though, aren't as interested in discretion.

👎 Top 10 Places Your Baby Doesn't Belong in Public

- A law school classroom
- Bars
- Dog fights
- Strip club
- Floor of the Stock Exchange
- Ski lift
- Shooting range
- Rave
- Airport smoking lounge
- Adult entertainment store

 Mindy Scott and I got a couple of dirty looks tonight at a restaurant from a couple of strangers after Nevaeh let out a brief piercing cry when she realized that the waitress brought everyone's food but the babbies'. Anyone have some good "put-em in their place" phrases for when people have a nasty attitude toward people with children?

about an hour ago • Like • Comment

> **Mindy** I was thinking along the lines of, "What's worse? For a baby to cry because he's hungry, or for adults to intentionally throw daggers with their eyes?" They minded their business afterward so I left them alone.
>
> about an hour ago • Like

> **Pamela** "If you had this waitress, you'd be doing the same thing."
>
> 25 minutes ago • Like

Sue I tend to flick corn or peas in their general direction . . . They stop staring then . . . but usually mumble something non-Christian as a result . . . Oh well.

8 minutes ago • Like

Servers should all be forced to wear shirts that say "Human Being" on them so that people like this can't forget that fact. Your server is a human. A person with two arms. She probably brought the adults' food out first because *that's what made sense*. Lay off the lady with the food, people. And remember to tip with something other than a dirty diaper.

 Kent Woman on the plane just changed her sons diaper while sitting next to me. What is proper flight etiquette in that situation?

6 hours ago • Like • Comment

> **George** Offer to hold the dirty diaper?
> 6 hours ago • Like 👍 3 people

> **April** Depends. You want the dirty diaper gone or smell it the entire flight?
> 6 hours ago • Like

> **Harvey** There's a changing table in the restroom, isn't there?
> 6 hours ago • Like

> **Kendra** Oh my! Not sure about that one!
> 6 hours ago • Like

> **Stuart** Melanie says the proper etiquette is to take the airplane magazine out of the seat back pocket and use it to fan the aroma away.
> 5 hours ago • Like

Denise Be patient with moms on the airplane! Its hard to fly with kids! The changing tables are useless on an airplane.

5 hours ago • Like

Andrew Gag, throw up and ask her for a baby wipe

5 hours ago • Like 👍 1 person

Charles Take the child to the restroom.

4 hours ago • Like

Laura I'm with Andrew on this one. Oh, and yes—have the Air Marshall give her a ticket.

4 hours ago • Like

Everyone knows that airplane bathroom stalls are a tight squeeze even without a baby, but if you can change your child on your lap, seat, or on an airplane tray (trays that are meant to be used as food trays, *barf*), then you can go to the (admittedly smelly) bathroom and change the baby there, too. The spaces are relatively comparable, and bathrooms exist for a reason no matter what age you are. Don't be the entitled ass who thinks everyone should be subjected to your child's poop just because you don't want to change him in the bathroom. If the plane goes down for an emergency landing, you'll be the last person who's offered any assistance from your fellow passengers. Just remember that.

Marissa Pimple face bitch at Dollar General pissed me off. Tyler had to pee and she wuldnt let him use the restroom! Wtf!

2 hours ago • Like • Comment

Skylar That's the way it was over at deer creek wouldn't unlock the door to restroom so grandma duncan just shit on floor lol

2 hours ago • Like

Marissa that's where i was. Luckily tyler held it long enough to make it to Kroger . . . but im still mad lol

2 hours ago • Like

Travis i would of took him to the back of the store and had him pee in an empty bottle and took it up to her and would of been like here i made you some lemonade lol

about an hour ago • Like 👍 2 people

If you take away one lesson from this book, let it be this: "When in doubt, especially in a Dollar General store, just shit on floor lol." Really, there is nothing more you need to know than that.

Risa . . . amazed at how many women walked in and out of the Walmart bathroom today while i struggled to clean up the WORST blow out diaper ive ever had!!!! . . . wow . . . were none of them mothers? did none of them have a spare few minutes to ask me if i needed help? And as i'm washing him with soap in the sink (yes it was THAT bad) one woman had the nerve to shoot me a dirty look and sigh as she walked out without washing her hands (in the empty sink next to me).

26 minutes ago • Like • Comment

Brittany Sorry you had to deal with that on your own, wish more people had your compassion and understanding for mothers.

23 minutes ago • Like

Carol Yup that's why I avoid that Walmart like the plague.

17 minutes ago • Like

Ellen :(I would let you change him at my house and leave poo on the driveway. ;) Mean people, I love you!!! I would have dove right in to help.

11 minutes ago • Like 👍 2 people

Jessica i would have gone to the baby isle and borrowed a changing pad and maybe a box of mega wipes. :) LOL! I would have helped you!!!

6 minutes ago • Like 👍 1 person

Susan :(. . . that is awful, people can be so selfish, unaware of anyone in need.

5 minutes ago • Like

Renee I've had those kind of blow outs all over a restaurant floor no fun

2 minutes ago • Like

Okay, so let me get this straight: If I'm shopping at Hell-on-Earth-Mart, and I take a break from my year-round Christmas shopping to use the facilities there, where I basically assume that everything I'm touching is already covered in "America's bacteria," I'm supposed to notice a random woman washing her baby in the sink and ask her if I can help her out? Like instead of just involuntarily getting covered in germs in a bathroom stall, I should voluntarily step in to assist someone whose son is covered in liquid diarrhea? And I should assume that she wants my help? This is all news to me!

24

Pregnancy and Labor

L ife, and parent overshare, begins at conception. Until just a few years ago, it wasn't typical (or practical) for a couple to tell hundreds of people that they're expecting a baby mere moments after seeing the results of a home pregnancy test, but today that's quickly becoming the norm. Now the list of things little girls dream of includes celebrating their sixteenth birthday, walking down the aisle on their wedding day, and announcing their pregnancy on Facebook.

In this world, anything goes. When a woman's hormones are out of whack, she can say whatever the hell she wants on the Internet. It's like the rule that applies to a pregnant woman eating whatever she wants in the real world applies to status updates in the online world. She will brazenly express her frustrations over her body, emotions, and the general public whether people want to hear her thoughts or not. And because she's getting acquainted with her body in gross and bizarre ways she never knew before pregnancy, she feels that everyone else should, too.

I don't know why so many people feel the need to share this level of detail about something so profoundly private, but it's a very common practice (more common than vaccination, actually!), and this chapter serves as an overview of everything pregnancy and labor related. Proceed with caution, and don't try this stuff at home.

 Tracie Coming in October . . . to a theatre near Tracie's vagina . . .
March 2 at 1:47pm • Like • Comment
👍 **2 people** like this.

The best thing about this announcement is that Tracie posted it herself. At first read, you might think for a second, "That dirtbag! Tracie's husband is a nasty bastard!" But then you go back to look at the poster's name, and yep, it still says Tracie. Talking about her vagina like it's a movie trailer. If you're wondering, I feel sufficiently grossed-out by the "theater screen's red curtains" joke that just ran through my mind.

 Tanya OMG GUESS WHAT? I DIDN'T WAIT THE SIX WEEKS TO HAVE SEX AND NOW IM PREGNANT AGAIN . . . OMG HOW CRAZY IS THAT??? IM EXCITED . . . I HOPE ITS A GIRL AND IF IT IS IM DONE . . .
about an hour ago via mobile • Like • Comment

Antoine Are you fuckin serious????
about an hour ago • Like

Tanya Yes sir . . . Congrats daddy . . .
about an hour ago • Like

Blake Tell me you didn't let your husband know via Facebook?
about an hour ago • Like

Tanya Yes sir . . . Lol . . .
about an hour ago • Like

This is one of those *STFU, Parents* blog submissions that I had to confirm with the submitter repeatedly because I was sure that it was fake. After being convinced of its authenticity, I cried into my hands awhile. But then I reconvinced myself that it's fake after all, so I can go on living my life pretending these people don't exist. Yay, denial!

Chelsie wishes she could just pick up her house a little without my uterus getting hard.
about an hour ago via mobile • Like • Comment

> **Brad** Someone was just saying, "I wonder how pliable Chelsie's uterus is today." Good thing you made it your status, so they don't have to wonder.
> 53 minutes ago • Like

> **Gwyneth** What was your excuse 6 months ago? LOL!
> 47 minutes ago • Like

> **Virginia** same thing happened to me from 21 weeks on when i was pregnant with dominic. made me very nervous!
> 45 minutes ago • Like

> **Heidi** Be cautious!
> 36 minutes ago • Like

> **Kelly** i know how u feel
> 31 minutes ago • Like

> **Adele** lol TMI Chelsie
> 26 minutes ago • Like

You know what really gets my goat? My hard-ass uterus. Bitch be getting hard if I just lean down to pick up the remote control! Forget about doing my laundry or the dishes. I swear, my uterus is the hardest, laziest organ EVER.

Angela just passed a piece of mucous plug! Yuck but yay!
18 minutes ago via mobile • Like • Comment

> **Diandra** Thanks for that info. . . . :/
> 10 minutes ago • Like

Every day the list of words that should never appear in one's status grows longer.

Patrick 6 cm mother fuckers
44 minutes ago via mobile • Like • Comment

> **Molly** what, your penis?
> 38 minutes ago • Like

> **Patrick** I just got owned! Nah 6cm is the size of the cervix my daughter is going to come out of
> 10 minutes ago • Like

> **Patrick** lightning crashes, a new mother cries her placenta falls to the floor the angel opens her eyes the confusion sets in before the doctor can even close the door
> about an hour ago via mobile • Like • Comment

In case you guys weren't sure, Patrick's wife is having a baby, and her cervix is 6 centimeters along. Also, this moment is emotional for Patrick so he's quoting (and possibly singing while quietly strumming a guitar in the delivery room) "Lightning Crashes," a song that topped the charts in 1994 and still carries significant meaning to this day (apparently). What a sensitive douche.

 Robyn Update for those interested: my wonderful midwife has just been and here's the latest—it wasn't my water that broke this morning, apparently I'm in the 25% of women who get a pre-labor "watery trickle," which is not the amniotic fluid. Good news is the cervix is Very soft (thanks raspberry leaf tea and evening primrose oil!) and I'm already dilated half-way without any contractions!!
46 minutes ago • Like • Comment

> **Robyn** So Baby will likely be with us very soon (by the end of the weekend at the very latest) and it looks like labor will very most likely be Very quick (hurray), which is what we like to hear!
> 44 minutes ago • Like 👍 2 people

> **Robyn** So now I'm going to have a nice relaxing bath and eat chocolate and drink more raspberry leaf tea =) hehe.
> 43 minutes ago • Like 👍 2 people

I'm going to put this as nicely as I can: Ladies, STOP TALKING ABOUT YOUR SOFT CERVIXES. I understand that a soft cervix is a good thing, and I understand what being dilated means, but what I *don't* understand is why moms-to-be think their friends want this much detail in their newsfeed. Can't they just say, "In a week or less the baby will finally be here!"? How hard is that? (No pun intended.)

25

Reminiscing Parents

The trend of parents taking a trip down memory lane—aka childbirth—on social media every time their kid celebrates a birthday was born purely out of the Facebook format. Story-hour-style memory dusting didn't exist back when pagers and Instant Messenger were the common ways of communicating "digitally" with friends. No one changed their AIM status or sent out a "mass page" every hour to publicly reflect on the year(s)-old birth of their child. I also doubt anyone ever sent out a page that said, "Guess what? Today is my baby's half birthday!" or "Guess what? Today is my baby's 247th day of life!," but I wouldn't know for sure since I was in high school at the time. (If anyone ever used a pager as a baby journal, I stand corrected.)

For whatever reason, some parents aren't satisfied with posting a concise "Happy birthday to my son, Caiden!" and moving on with their day. They must include some other detail—or dozens of details—to sufficiently convey the significance of the day. Not to mention, birthdays are so important to modern-day parents, they've managed to loosen the definition and guidelines for what even constitutes a birthday. Back in the day, it was defined as the day one was born. If it wasn't that day, well, then it wasn't your birthday. The Mad Hatter in *Alice in Wonderland* even coined the term "unbirthday" to represent all of the other days of the year that a person wasn't celebrating being a year older. But nowadays, a person could feasibly have a birthday for every *week* of his or her existence. Aren't babies lucky!

 Joyce Two years ago today, I married the man of my dreams. And one year ago today, we made Addison!
4 minutes ago via mobile • Like • Comment

Wham, bam, thank ya, ma'am! Milestones R Us! It's Joyce's Conception Day and she couldn't wait to let everyone know that one year ago *today* she was getting it on with her husband and then they made a baby! And now that baby is almost three months old and it's officially time to reminisce! Yay :)

 Lindsay 5 years ago today (as of 8am) I was in labor! To be continued . . .
28 minutes ago via mobile • Like • Comment
👍 **3 people** like this.

"To be continued . . ." may be the scariest three words an update can contain, particularly if the big "story" is reliving a friend's five-year-old labor.

JoAnn Today is Mackenzie Isabella's B-day . . . ♥ 12 yrs ago today I was having a emergency C sec ~ ♪♫♪ Happy Birthday ♪♫♪ Mackenzie I love you!!!!!!!!!!!!!!!11

6 hours ago via mobile • Like • Comment

Talk about your grab bag of status updates. There's heartfelt emotion, heart emoticons, an exclamation point (or two) to represent every year Mackenzie's been alive, a quick mention of a "C sec" (hip lingo), *and* musical notes! It's like a modern-day "Happy Birthday" song!

Cortney Well one year ago our sweet little Caleb came tearing thru my vjayjay and def was one of the most intense days of my life. Caleb is one of the most special people I know. This boy will do great things . . . Yes, Caleb a very happy birthday to you!

1 hour ago via mobile • Like • Comment

👍 **2 people** like this.

". . . tearing thru my vjayjay." Cortney had good intentions when she used that phrasing. You know she did.

26

Sanctimommy

Becoming a sanctimommy (that is, a sanctimonious mother) is practically a rite of passage. It means that as a parent, you're enlightened. You've begun to mentally divide the world up into various compartments, and you'll never see anything the same way again. From the moment you become a sanctimommy (or the elusive sanctidaddy!), people will be split into two categories: "Us" and "Them." "Us" is the group that comprises all parents. You know, all the people who take on the immense responsibility of raising tomorrow's generation of thought leaders and crackheads and then generously sacrifice their own hobbies and friendships for those of their children.

"Them" is basically everyone else, and as a nonparent, you either "get" that or you don't. No childfree individual is going to understand what it's like to be a parent or have the ability to see the world through the eyes of a child.

Noah Only when you are a parent you realize how life is worth more with a child.

17 minutes ago • Like • Comment

Only when you are a sailor you realize how vast the ocean is. Only when you are a mime you realize how much other people talk. Only when you are sanctimonious do you realize how many people can't stand you since you had a child.

 Stephanie I am making a human being today, what did you do?

2 hours ago via mobile • Like • Comment

👍 **6 people** like this.

> **Melissa** Been there, done that!! Lol
>
> 2 hours ago • Like 👍 1 person

> **Jana** You're an amazing creature who was made for creation.
>
> about an hour ago • Like 👍 1 person

> **Stephanie** We all are :) How amazing is that!
>
> about an hour ago • Like 👍 1 person

Ahhh, who doesn't like a little self-righteousness with their over-share? Personally, I find one to be incredibly lacking without the other. It's like having a Jewish grandmother without the nagging!

 Maria I am a stay at home mom, I love what I do. it's not a job to me, but a preference, a way of life, just because I stay at home does not mean that I sit on the couch eating bon-bons and watching soaps all day. I "work" harder than many of you with jobs. I would make a hefty wager that after one day in my shoes (or any mom who stays at home) you would be ready to go back to work. I love being a stay at home mom!

5 hours ago via mobile • Like • Comment

👍 **2 people** like this.

Maria I just beat the computer at Scrabble by 100 points!!
hell yeah! :)

3 hours ago • Like 👍 1 person

Being a stay-at-home mom is hard work. Cooking, cleaning, wiping baby butts, and generally getting shit done is not the easy-peasy cakewalk some people think it is. Heck, sometimes they do so much *stuff* that goes unnoticed and unappreciated, they just want to go on strike! So, to everyone who's not a stay-at-home mom, please don't whine about how hard your job is—especially considering moms don't get sick days OR vacation.

OMG! OMG! TRIPLE WORD SCORE!!!! BOO-YA, computer!!!

Lora Dear friends, I love that you invite me to so many lovely things. My children are an extension of me and are a part of our community. Please expect that they will be with me at events and plan accordingly. Please welcome them with starting things on time, having space for them to move around in if a lot of people are there, toys and snacks if possible, and people to hang out with them or with me with them as they are still quite little. Please make announcements at the beginning of events even if you don't see children present that children's presence and noise is welcomed and that folks should speak up and be conscientious. Please offer child care for every event without being asked. Please introduce yourself to me and my kids before touching them, picking them up, or going off to play. They are little, yes, but they are people who are a part of the community and deserve inclusion and respect.

I will not leave them at home. I usually can't leave them at home. Please keep inviting me to your events, and please keep this in mind.

about an hour ago • Like • Comment

👍 **11 people** like this.

> **Lora** No friends this is not in response to any particular thing, nothing happened per se, just tired.
>
> about an ago • Like

> **Kay** well, I hope you come to birthday brunch on Sunday—helpful people, toys and snacks included
>
> about an ago • Like

> **Sarabeth** May 22 12:30-3 Tristyn's 3rd birthday party, swimming optional afterwards, face painting, games n fun for all.
>
> about an ago • Like

> **Hannah** Love this. Thank you.
>
> about an ago • Like 👍 1 person

FINALLY, someone says what's on everybody's mind! KIDS ARE PART OF OUR COMMUNITY. They are part of our world. They are small people who sometimes do not know how to form sentences or drive cars or walk more than a few feet without falling down, but they are PEOPLE, people!

27

Spoiled Brats

Nothing's more annoying than being around a spoiled child. But coming in a close second has got to be watching the development of a spoiled child via your friends' social media feeds. Your friends are friends with *you*, not your children, so while it's nice to hear updates about a person's kids, those status updates should be selective and thoughtful.

But regardless of what parents post about their kids, above all the updates are reflections of them and their parenting methods. I think a lot of parents tend to forget that fact, but the truth is, posts about people's kids are windows into a family's lifestyle. And if that lifestyle involves piles of gifts on every holiday, supersized vanilla fudge milkshakes at 8 a.m., and long-winded stories about bitching out a server for telling your child that he couldn't throw silverware, your friends are going to think you're raising one hell of a shithead.

Cheri Why is it that my 2 year old son has his own $300 phone and still insists on playing with mine . . .

2 hours ago • Like • Comment

> **Allison** Cause its mommys so its better
>
> 2 hours ago • Like

> **Wendy** Because hes 2 and wants everything mommy has
>
> about an hour ago • Like

What can Demi say? The boy likes luxury! Plus, if you think about it, every little kid should have his or her own $300 phone. It totally keeps kids occupied, and it keeps them from wanting to play with other people's phones. Wait . . . no, it doesn't.

Naomi Opening an account for Nathan and the banker is just in shock as Memphus destroys his office all I can do is laugh

5 hours ago • Like • Comment

👍 **4 people** like this.

> **Naomi** I mean destroy . . . he took his name plate and threw it with all his business cards . . . then took all his pamphlets n threw them on the floor . . . well he was picking up his business cards and the guy asks Memphus do u need to sit down and Memphus gave him the look
>
> 5 hours ago • Like

> **Christine** Lmfao it's because Memphus is just so stinking cute!
>
> 5 hours ago • Like

Oh, *Memphus*, that lovably misspelled chap who can't keep his little hands to himself in places of business! What an absolute scamp.

Only a child as adorable as Memphus can get away with such mayhem at the bank! He just loves to test people. It's hilarious.

 Loki Adorabelle calls it like it is . . . She addressed us by saying "hello servant" tonight.

9 hours ago • Like • Comment

👍 **Sarah and Koa** like this.

> **Nina** nice.
>
> 9 hours ago • Like
>
> ___
>
> **Fiona** OMG!!! \ (*o*) /
>
> 8 hours ago • Like
>
> ___
>
> **Kelly** Wow . . . already ruling the house
>
> 4 hours ago • Like
>
> ___
>
> **Monique** Sooo funny! Will be fun (?) as she grows up!
>
> 3 hours ago • Like

Here are some precious things that come out of children's smart mouths:

- "Hello, servant."
- "I don't want the cereal in the white China. I want it in the IVORY CHINA!"
- "Can you tell me the Paris Hilton story again, Mommy?"
- "NO, four is NOT too young to get facial injectables! UGGHHH, you don't understand anything!!!"

Kids these days!

Adriana December is my hijo's birthday month. He will be 5 on the 27, so everyday of the month of December Mateo gets what ever he wants, so today for breakfast he had Toaster Strudels, and a Root Beer float. His Daddy gets him everything toys, candy, movies, video games Every day. He is the only 4 year old I know with a flat screen in his room! All because of Daddy

Yesterday at 9:18am • Like • Comment

Is this kid getting a heart attack for his birthday? I'm all about throwing a special treat in a child's direction when he/she does well in an area of importance, but feeding a kid an entire bag of granulated sugar just for having a birthday and then sending him off to school is criminal. "All because of Daddy," my ass. Adriana's pantry must be *leaking* diabetes.

28

Story Hour

Every so often, a status update is so long-winded and so tedious to read, it qualifies for the Status Olympics (part of the International Games that I'm sure Facebook is creating as we speak). Most parent overshare has to do with not having any filter, but Story Hour specifically refers to people who don't have an inner editor. They go on and on, either in a single status update or in a series of updates, explaining in excruciating detail just how much laundry they did when their child was sick or *exactly* how they spent their afternoon at the zoo in a minute-by-minute recap.

It'd be easy to say that you know a Story Hour update when you see one, because a typical example looks like big blocks of rambling text, all written by the same person. But not all Story Hours are the same. Each one is nuanced and irritating for different reasons, most of them impressively tiring. While perhaps many people have been tempted to write paragraph-long status updates about how many words their kid knows, most of us have the good sense to fight that urge. But not all of us, which is a damn shame.

 Charlene well . . . went and got shayley from school, went to daniel's dads, went back to the school and picked up chastity and korin then went to the store to get a couple of things and they didn't even have the main thing i needed (diapers) so was going to go to kroger but had such a horrible tooth ache that i just came home and am hoping owen has enough diapers to last till i take the girls to school in the morning. was going to make biscuits and sausage gravy for dinner until i opened the ground sausage and realized that it looked like paste rather than meat, threw that away and am now making a skillet meal then working before watching greys anatomy
February 20 at 6:36pm • Like • Comment

 Charlene worked about 2 hours today, gonna work maybe another hour later, gotta go pick up shayley, run a couple errands and pick korin and chastity up from their after school program, then home for some homeschooling work for the kids, dinner, laundry, dishes and work . . . and greys tonight :)
February 20 at 2:40pm • Like • Comment

Charlene's version of Story Hour is like the C-SPAN of status updates. Endlessly boring, endearingly dated, and completely ignored by anyone pretending to care. Also a lot like *Grey's Anatomy* in that way, although *Grey's Anatomy* at least has mildly interesting cliffhangers. Charlene's stories are just a long, flat dirt road.

Jeneanne Our son is by far AMAZING! Every single person I speak with from strangers, to daycare, family, friends, co-workers, . . . talk about how smart he is! He is saying probably around 200 words! Everything we say and do he copies. He sings A, B for ABC's. He touches his diaper when he is going potty. He says all animal noises. He knows every part of his face. He knows who every1 in the fam is. Seaseme Street characters. Dances. Sings. Vacuums with his when I do with mine.

Yesterday at 4:57pm • Like • Comment

👍 **6 people** like this.

Jeneanne Mama, mommy, mom, daddy, dada, papa, gramma, nana, nanu, an lana for auntie lana, bo for uncle bob, wa wa for water, wa wa for his pacifier, elmo, bert, growls for cookie monster . . . dinosaurs . . . and bears, A B for abc's, bubba bath for bubble bath, glitter, airplane everytime one flys by, hecopter for helicopter, book, toys, outsy for outside, up, yuck, mmm for yum, egg, mil for milk, juice, appa juice for apple juice, vrrrmmm for car, more, all done, nanna for banana, apple, ithe for ice (lisp there lol), sss for shoe and swing and slide and sand, cup, dirt, ... says wa wa when he sees a sprinkler even when it is off,

Yesterday at 5:02pm • Like

Jeneanne He takes a straw out of his juice box and Capri Sun and is able to put it back into that little tiny whole right away, puts lids back on in one try, scoops bark into a pot using a baby shovel, runs, says bat and ball and hits the ball with the bat, when I ask him to open or close a door or bring me something he does it, points to his pee pee and says pee pee even if he is peeing in the bath tub, scribbles on paper to color, picks up his food with his fork and puts it in his mouth, takes off part of his seat belt on his own (can be a bad thing

I know), brushes his own teeth every single day and says teeee,

Yesterday at 5:07pm • Like

Jeneanne Says rock and throws it, kicks a soccer ball, spins in circles to copy his cousin dancing like a ballerina,. . . dona with bottles . . . just need to work on the pacifier. POINT IS, HE IS AMAZING!!!! ♥

Yesterday at 5:08pm • Like

Jeneanne P.s. HE IS ONLY 15 MONTHS OLD!

Yesterday at 5:12pm • Like

Jeneanne is like a talking toy that's sputtering out of control. "Seaseme [*sic*] Street!" "Hecopter!" "A B for ABC's!" "Ithe!" "SSSS FOR SHOE!" "MY KID SPINS IN CIRCLES AND IS FREAKING AMAZING!!!"

Beth Yes, my life revolves around this baby right now. I did leave the house yesterday for about an hour (Library, Grocery, Pizza) but that's not nearly as exciting as the fact that her cord scab is hanging by a thread and when it falls off we are going to take a BAAAATH together! Yay!

about an hour ago • Like • Comment

Beth In related news, Sage threw up all over both of us today. Given the quantity of barely digested breast milk that came shooting up out of her, Exorcist-style, I have no doubts about my milk supply. Also, it must be tasty, because someone did NOT know when she had had enough. *sigh* I am all too familiar with this problem.

about an hour ago • Like

Rosemary She's cute and everything but babies are gross

about an hour ago • Like

The "One More Thing" Story Hour example is a common one. A parent launches into a story about one thing in her status update, but then recalls an entirely different—and yet equally entertaining and important—story with which to follow it up. In reality, neither story should have ever made it onto Facebook. Clues include words like "cord scab," "BAAAATH," "barely digested," and *Exorcist*-style." Paired together, those words are either part of a gruesome play about a scab-eating zombie, *or* they're part of a story that shouldn't be told online. That may sound harsh, but the truth hurts sometimes.

 Kiera Had a wonderful multi-kid/multitasking moment today. Sent both girls to go potty while I tooke my laundry out of the dryer. All of a sudden I heard mommy Poo-Poo with great cheer. Chloe was waiting for me to wipe her and Briella took it upon herself to personally let me know she went in her potty. Warning TMI . . . Briella pooped so much that a piece was stuck to her butt and she left it on the floor for me to pick up.

Yesterday at 3:52pm • Like • Comment

> **Kiera** I am so glad that overnight Briella has been very good at potty training. We are going on three days with no accidents. I just need to teach her to wait for someone to wipe her before she gets up from now on. ARGH!
>
> Yesterday at 3:54pm • Like

> **Debbie** Oh the joys of having kids. If you have kids nothing is TMI anymore!
>
> Yesterday at 4:55pm • Like

"If you have kids nothing is TMI anymore!" WRONG. That is wrong. Whoever thinks it's perfectly fine to post on the Internet about a *piece of poop* that was stuck to *a child's butt* and wound up getting LEFT ON THE FLOOR has got problems. This isn't up for debate.

29

Super Mom

It's a bird! It's a plane! It's . . . !!! Well, you know. Fucking Super Mom. She's always there to tell you about her many superpowers, like shooting enough milk from her breasts to feed a small army (of children); multitasking by juggling laundry, homework, poopy diapers, and Farmville; and growing and giving birth to human life. What did yooooou do today? Super Moms *did it all*. She cooked, she cleaned, she fed, she bathed, she kissed boo-boos, wiped asses, piloted a fighter jet, single-handedly saved the world from total destruction, *und* somehow managed to eat a banana. Can you compete with that? I didn't think so.

Janet i find my superpower to be quite exceptional.. i can grow a baby BOY inside me. doesn't that blow your mind in the slightest? i mean really, the miracle of life is simply amazing.

Wednesday at 11:30pm • Like • Comment

👍 **11 people** like this.

Arie Pretty dang extraordinary lil mama! Congrats on the boy!
Thursday at 12:35am • Like

Lola Actually, I think it's amazing. After growing two girls, the thought of growing a boy inside me (a girl!) is kiiiiind of crazy and mildly absurd. So yes, that's amazing.
Thursday at 8:02am• Like

Ally Then after you have the baby, your superpower is making milk with you, well you get the idea. . . .
Thursday at 4:53pm • Like 👍 1 person

Anna baby boys are awesome congrats!
16 hours ago • Like

Oooh, FANCY. A boy penis growing inside of a female body. Talk about exceptional. All I've done lately that's exceptional is *finally* removed a bunch of Food Network programming from my DVR after coming to the realization that I'm never going to watch any of it. Pretty dang extraordinary if you ask me!

Margie today Wyatt told me he loved me, but still wished I was a superhero
23 minutes ago • Like • Comment
👍 **3 people** like this.

Barbara any woman that pushes a kiddo out her vagina is a superhero. He'll understand one day that you're Wonder Woman.
18 minutes ago • Like

Giving birth is by far the easiest way for a woman to become a superhero. In fact, all it takes to be Wonder Woman is a baby and a vagina!

Chrstyal Words NOT to wake up to: Mama, my diaper came off and I accidentally made a mess on the floor. Really squishy— Sigh. And I was having a dream about being a super hero. Guess I really am one.

3 hours ago • Like • Comment

👍 **Cindy and Tera** like this.

> **Jenny** definitely a super hero!
>
> 3 hours ago • Like

All I hear in my head when I read this is Eeyore's voice from Winnie-the-Pooh. "Here I was dreaming about being a superhero. Guess I really am one. Don't pay any attention to me, guys. Nobody ever does. *WOMP WOMP WAHHHHHHMP.*"

Ilana if you had a super power what would it be?! humor me . . .

3 hours ago • Like • Comment

> **Brooke** Invisibility. Second choice would be flying
>
> 3 hours ago • Like

> **Cole** Whatever the power is called where you can travel from one place to another (any other ol' place you want) in the BLINK OF AN EYE!
>
> 3 hours ago • Like

> **Alexandra** Reading and controlling minds! Or super strength would be sweet.
>
> 3 hours ago • Like

Ellen I do have one! ;) I make milk that sustains life.

Waaaaait a second: Is Ellen trying to say that she *naturally* makes MILK—and then uses it to *keep a human being alive?!* Is that really what I just read? Because if so, that is just incredible. Also, I don't believe her. I'm sorry, but does Ellen appreciate how implausible that sounds? I'd probably believe she has telekinesis or that she can walk through walls before I believed that she could make milk and sustain life with it. There's just no fuckin' way. I even looked it up and couldn't find a single example of another person who's able to do this, including people with special psychic powers. Good try, though. She almost had me. "I make milk that sustains life . . ." Lol, *suuure* she does!

30

Teen-Related Overshare

The majority of parent overshare is about babies and toddlers because the updates are written by people with younger children. Parents with older kids tend not to overshare as much because they've already raised their children for years without revealing every detail of their kids' lives on social media—but that doesn't mean there aren't some who still do. Lots, actually. And if you're over the age of eleven, you can probably guess what they're posting about.

Now life is all about girls getting their periods, boys masturbating in the shower, and everyone growing hair in their armpits. There aren't as many parents who post about these things, which is good considering their children are old enough to have their own social media accounts and read their parents' updates themselves in their newsfeeds.

For those kids whose parents *do* share stories about their adolescent development, I wish I could tell them that it happens to everyone, and that each of us has been through that type of humiliation growing up. I wish I could say that my mother hired a skywriter to write, "Blair's First Period!!!! She is a woman now!!!!" across the sky when I was in seventh grade, and plastered the city with flyers about my brother's pubic hair and acne when he was sixteen. But I can't, because that would have been totally fucked up. My mother would never do that, nor would she ever "break news" about my physical changes on the Internet, so really I just feel bad for people whose parents do that to them now.

 Gabby OMGoodness, My daughter has "officially" begun puberty! She is only 10 years old and tells me after school today that she started her period at school yesterday . . . Then the little turkey Bonnie proceeds to tell everyone in the neighborhood so Shanna had to keep denying it to the kids outside! Poor Shanna!
9:51pm • Like • Comment

Show of hands, ladies! Who wishes their mom had sent a virtual newsletter to everyone she knows after hearing about your first period? I know I do.

Alisha Tomorrow is Noam's first day of 6th grade and last night we discovered his first chin hair! He may be small, but he is going to be able to grow a mean beard just like his grandpa!!! He is SO excited . . .
14 minutes ago • Like • Comment

OMG, you guys, Noam is *super* stoked to discover that any day now, he's going to be able to grow a killer beard just like his grandpa! He's just gotten his first chin hair at age eleven, so probably by the end of the school year or so, he'll be rocking a mean old beard just like ol' Gramps! Oh man, is he excited . . . Beards are such a gift for a little boy.

 Dolores For all who care, my son has about 15 armpit hairs!!
16 minutes ago • Like • Comment
👍 **Melissa** likes this.

> **Melissa** lol! how old is he?
> 15 minutes ago • Like

> **Dolores** 14 :)
> 15 minutes ago • Like

> **Kirin** Hopefully your oldest!
> 14 minutes ago • Like

> **Dolores** Lol!!
> 14 minutes ago • Like

> **Agyness** @Kirin—LMAO!
> 10 minutes ago • Like

> **Britt** mazel tov
> 10 minutes ago • Like

> **Dolores** He just had me look very closely!
> 9 minutes ago • Like

> **Mandy** yay Jasper! And to say, I knew you when . . .
> 5 minutes ago • Like

Dolores's playful announcement shows that she is aware that her update is ridiculous, but that doesn't mean she's exempt from the Parents' Law of Body Hair Discussion, which expressly bans the mention of an adolescent's body hair regardless of region. Just because a kid—excuse me, *man*—tells his mom that he's sprouting armpit hair doesn't mean he wants her to tell the whole world about it. I almost feel like rolling my eyes in Dolores's direction and rebelling on her son's behalf. Who wants to dye their hair blue and get their eyebrow pierced?

Stella I know I should be glad my 14yr old takes a shower, but I am going to have to buy a shower timer that turns off in 10mins. I can only think she must be shaving her legs in there. 20mins and counting.

6 hours ago • Like • Comment

> **Jenifer** LOL :) I remember those days. I'm thinking you may be right about the shaving. Are you going to put her on restriction when she gets out..?? LOL :-p
>
> 6 hours ago • Like

> **Cecily** My 15 yr old is in there forever too . . . only he's a BOY! Can't imagine how he'd need that long to bathe . . .
>
> 6 hours ago • Like

> **Hillary** Um . . . Cecily . . . they aren't washing for 20 minutes . . . at least this was a confession of my 13 year old boy. I mean.. I'm glad he feels like he can TALK to me.. but.. come on.. I DON'T NEED TO KNOW THAT!
>
> 5 hours ago • Like

> **Loren** Wait until she starts taking 2 or 3 a day! That's something I could never understand about my sister.
>
> 5 hours ago • Like

> **Cecily** oh Hillary . . . I'm all too aware of what transpires, my boy hasn't a filter with me either. . . .
>
> 5 hours ago • Like

I love the way Hillary says that her son feels like he can talk to her about his "showering" habits. Well, not anymore, bitch! Don't these people realize their kids—and all of their kids' friends—have social media profiles, too? And that discussing a teenager's masturbation routine on the Internet is worse than posting his nude baby pictures? This is how revolutions start.

31

The Joys of Parenting!

Like any job, motherhood has its share of ups and downs. But unlike most corporate jobs—or any job with a boss, really—motherhood is the one that women are supposed to cherish and give gratitude for on a daily basis. While it's normal for overworked executives or assistants to say, "Ugh, I hate my job today!," mothers tend to do the opposite. Rather than curse the shit out of their frustrations, some moms feel the urge to feign joy, whether it's to be funny or out of guilt. After all, it's wrong to despise your job if your job is looking after your baby . . . isn't it? (Real answer: no.) Well, according to some moms on Facebook, it is.

And that's where the expression "the joys of motherhood" comes into play. Those four little words creep into more status updates written by moms than I can count. Women cling to them as a humorous way to offset just about any complaint imaginable. Kids screaming on an airplane? The joys of motherhood! Baby experienced a blowout during church? The joys of motherhood! It's another way of saying, "You don't know [sleep/love/pride/scuba diving] until you're a mom!," except with less 'tude. Plus, using the expression at the end of a status update allows mothers to vent about practically anything. So long as it's backed up with that catchall phrase, or someone says it in a comment, moms can bitch about floaters, "breast-milk poops," "up-the-back" blowouts, and projectile diarrhea without so much as flinching.

 Jess Definition of 'the joys of motherhood.' On route to make your jam on toast and discovering the biggest smelliest turd. Is 'blockin' your toilet . . . even after still 4 flushes an a coat hanger pushed down . . . on the upside atleast the culpret no longer has 'blocked.' Bowels !!!!!!!!
Friday at 2:20pm • Like • Comment
👍 **Karly** likes this.

> **Jess** An the jam on toast was yummmmmy !!!
> Friday at 2:30pm • Like

Who else is relieved to hear that Jess's jam on toast was still delicious? Thank goodness! I wouldn't want the joys of motherhood to get in the way of *Jess's* appetite. Good thing the Renaissance woman was able to solve her coat hanger–prodded "culpret" problem *and* enjoy a tasty snack, unlike the rest of the people reading her update at their desks during lunch.

Kathleen There is nothing like the feeling of warm spit-up sliding down the inside of your pajama sleeve and oozing the whole way past your elbow at 7 a.m. to start the day. Ugh!

3 hours ago • Like • Comment

👍 **Patrick** likes this.

> **Jessie** Yuck! Kaylee spit up one time down my back and it ozzed down in my underwear and on my ass :p
>
> 3 hours ago • Like
>
> ---
>
> **Bianca** I remember those days :) Aaaahhhh . . . the joys of motherhood!
>
> 2 hours ago • Like
>
> ---
>
> **Kate** The best is in the middle of the night and you're too tired to clean it up, and when you wake up you wonder what that awful smell is!
>
> 2 hours ago • Like

We've got oozing, we've got ozzing, and then to cap it off, Julie admits to dozing while covered in vomit. Which, if you think about it, most people have probably done at some point in their lives, but the difference is that Julie is the one laughing about it online.

If these are the joys of motherhood, I'd like to kindly ask that moms keep the shitty parts of motherhood off social media. I don't think I can handle whatever those might be.

Shelby . . . liquid poop all over my thigh from a leaky diaper. Looks like Thai yellow curry—mmmmm

3 hours ago • Like • Comment

👍 **Gwen** likes this.

Julie hahahaha!! I know that's sooo wrong, yet it made me laugh out loud . . . ah, the joys of motherhood. One day I'll get there . . . one day. lol

3 hours ago • Like

Eva lol, i think someone's eating yellow curry in the office right now

3 hours ago • Like

Lydia ewwwww . . . I don't miss that part! :)

3 hours ago • Like

Nichelle Yet again, another thank you for proving to be a wonderful form of birth control for me! ♥

3 hours ago • Like

Dustin Hey wait till it is coming out both ends

2 hours ago • Like

Gwen no more curry for you!!!

2 hours ago • Like

Donna Wow! You're are mom for sure now when you can compare baby poop to yummy food.

14 minutes ago • Like

This is a "joys of parenting" / "poop" / "you know you're a mom when" hybrid, and the thing that binds them all is "Thai yellow curry poop." Talk about your nasty adhesives.

Once again, adding "mmmm" to your liquid poop updates does not make them any more palatable or amusing. Especially when curry is involved.

Emilie is covered in poo from the poo fountain that came out of Riley's little bottom!

56 minutes ago • Like • Comment

👍 **6 people** likes this.

> **Arianna** lol. Oh the joy . . .
>
> 42 minutes ago • Like

Arianna didn't even finish writing out "the joys of motherhood" because this is just so obviously NOT A JOY. Or at least, that's what I'm telling myself. Because there is no joy in Emilie's story. There's no crying in baseball, and there's no joy in poo fountains.

32

Woe Is Mom

Some people can't help but complain on social media. I like to believe social networking is all about sharing stories, news items, and significant events with friends, but many people use it as a platform to throw themselves pity parties. And while I think it would be difficult to find a person who *hasn't* ever complained online before (about traffic, work stress, or simply having a bad day), there's one type of person out there whose complaining doesn't get much pity from me: the Woe Is Mom.

According to a Woe Is Mom, life is SO. HARD. Even the minutest problems can seem monumentally important. People not paying attention to your baby, or people paying *too much* attention to your baby, or simply ignoring the fact that babies have to sleep at odd hours during the day when neighbors tend to do yard work.

Sometimes a Woe Is Mom is woeful because of all the things she used to be able to do before she had kids, like brush her teeth, change her underwear, and watch Kathie Lee and Hoda in the mornings while sipping a glass of chardonnay. When you have a baby, life is always go, go, go, and so many people simply do not understand that. They think being a mom to a baby is as easy is being a mom to a cat, but FYI, *it's not*. Don't test a Woe Is Mom or get in her way, because you *will* get smothered in shouts, tears, and rage, and it will not be easy to shake off. The Woe Is Mom has a comeback for *everything*.

Jamie I smell fall outside, makes me want to curl up by the fire with a good book . . . But I can't, because i'm a mom!

about an hour ago via mobile • Like • Comment

👍 **Ashley** likes this.

Kit I love this time of year . . . the rain feels great . . . bring on some college football!!!!!

about an hour ago • Like

Jamie I wish, we have sports, sports, sports all day . . .

about an hour ago • Like

For your consideration, a list of things that women cannot do in the fall once they become mothers (in case there was any confusion):

- Curl up by the fire with a good book
- Roast marshmallows (unless the marshmallows are for her children)
- Wear scarves (they take way too much time to tie)
- Pick apples
- Watch college football

But mothers don't have time to "read" or "relax" regardless of season, so don't go thinking these are fun activities that moms don't do in the fall but manage to make up for in the winter. Ohhh no. Moms just can't do certain seasonal things, and that's the way it is. Like any affliction, they deal with it every single day when they're reminded that life became a little less awesome when they decided to become a parent.

 Lisa Ugh! Thanks gardener next door . . . you woke up my kid after an hour. Are you going to come hang out with him while he is cranky all day? Nope, didn't think so. Thanks a lot.
16 minutes ago • Like • Comment

Hey, Mr. Gardener, I've got a question for ya. Are *you* going to come hang out with my grating son when he's cranky all day? Are *you* going to quietly cry to yourself after hiding in a closet just to avoid being around your own child? No? I didn't think so. Thanks for making life a living hell, Mr. Gardener. Real swell. I hope my neighbor's flowers look fucking spectacular.

 Michele Dear fire department,

I think It's great that u fight fires for people but I'm confused at why u need crazy loud sirens? They wake up my baby and I do not appreciate them.

Sincerely,

Annoyed momma
26 minutes ago via mobile • Like • Comment
👍 **3 people** likes this.

Liz I agree totally. Siren should be for emergency so we can get our kids and get in a safe place or something useful. To dang loud!!!!!

22 minutes ago via mobile • Like

OMG, can firefighters not just use some kind of dog-whistle-type thing when there's a fire so they can prevent a *different* type of emergency—waking up a baby?! Think about it: If a mother and her baby don't get enough sleep because of fire engine sirens, that will make them both tired the next day. That means the chances of the mom forgetting she has something in the oven increase considerably, which means her chances of starting a fire increase, too. And *that* means the fire department is working harder than they need to and spending unnecessary tax dollars! So really, it's in *everyone's* best interest to stop using those loud and disruptive sirens! To [sic] dang loud!!!

 Maura dear do-gooders of the world: Do NOT, I repeat, DO NOT ring my doorbell during naptime. I will find you and make it hurt, big time. And then, when I answer the door with a growling, barking dog behind me and a screaming 2 year old—under no circumstances is it appropriate to pitch your issue to me. Next time, the dog gets a snack. GRRRRRRR

about an hour ago • Like • Comment

👍 **2 people** likes this.

> **Calliope** HAHAHAHA!
> about an hour ago via mobile • Like
>
> **Becca** LOVE THIS!
> about an hour ago via mobile • Like

Do-gooders! Stop trying to save the world DURING NAPTIME!! Did you not see the Excel spreadsheet Maura put on the front door detailing her baby's sleep schedule? She's said it once, and she'll say it again: Whales do not need to be saved while the baby is sleeping!

33

You Know You're a Mom When . . .

Y ou know you're a mom when" is a lot like "the joys of motherhood" but with a different set of words. It has the exact same purpose and meaning, but with a slightly more self-deprecating bent. When a mom says, "The joys of motherhood!" she's really saying, "The joys of this non-paying shitfest we call motherhood!" It's more of a resigned response to something happening that's out of her control. But when a mom says, "You know you're a mom when" she's really saying, "Listen to the wacky and disgusting thing I did that's related to parenting that was sort of within my control, but I was so freaking *exhausted* that I hardly realized it! Do you feel me, moms?! Holler if you've ever gone grocery shopping in an oversized gray sweatshirt that was covered in vomit, ladies!!!"

And much like the way women automatically start saying "mama" to refer to themselves and their friends the second after they get pregnant, "you know you're a mom when" is one of those unavoidable terms that just comes naturally to mothers. It's like when bad expressions happen to good people. It's also used as a precursor to saying something confessional that would otherwise sound disgusting and out of place. By adding "you know you're a mom when," mothers allow themselves the freedom to confess something gross under the false guise of humor. Unfortunately for them, it doesn't seem to be working.

Camie You know you're a mom when: your son pees on your pants and you just let it dry. If that's not motherly love idk what is!

7 minutes ago • Like • Comment

Hmm, I don't know Camie. That's close to motherly love, but a *real* mother who loves her son would take off those pants, circle the part where he peed with a permanent marker, and take them to a craft store to get professionally mounted in a shadowbox. Now *that* is love.

Amanda You know you're a real momma when you accidentally smear baby poop on your jeans, wipe it off with a baby wipe, and then tell yourself that your pants are clean. Yep. That's me.

2 hours ago • Like • Comment

👍 **19 people** likes this.

> **Taylor** Yeah . . . I've definitely done that.
> about an hour ago • Like

> **Sarah** I am seriously laughing out loud and busting my gut right now! Awesome!
> about an hour ago • Like

> **Josephine** Been there sister!!! :)
> 47 minutes ago • Like

Hahaha, wearing your child's poop is supposed to be "gross," but when you're a real momma it is actually kind of hilarious! You don't even bother changing pants anymore after the first or second time it happens. Plus, they're called "mom jeans" for a reason, people. And that reason is that the denim is stretched in such a way to obscure baby shit and essentially camouflage any preexisting diarrhea from clear visibility.

Shari You know you are a mommy when you find crusty, baby boogers on your I-phone and it really doesn't bother you!
2 hours ago • Like • Comment
👍 **7 people** likes this.

> **Zack** Yuck!!!!
> 2 hours ago • Like

Remember back in the early 2000s when everyone got their phone blinged out with flashy little rhinestones? Well, Shari's phone is like that, except instead of rhinestones, her phone is covered in crusty boogers. They don't have the same sparkle, but they sure make a statement!

Anita You know you are a true mom, who really loves your kids when, instead of changing the sheets on your bed because the nap time pull-up leaked, you just get out your blow dryer and dry the spot!!!!!
March 30 at 8:25pm via mobile • Like • Comment
👍 **Stacie and 5 others** likes this.

> **Jill** Ugggg! Is that what I have to look forward to one day? LOL
> March 30 at 8:32pm • Like

Shanye lol mine slept in my bed the other night and for some reason i woke up and there was a huge wet spot, he was soaked, i had to put him in the tub it was so bad, my fault for not making him go before bed!! ugh sucks!!!

March 30 at 8:32pm • Like

Anita Jill, that is nothing!!! You'll see???

March 30 at 9:09pm • Like

Justine Didn't that take longer though . . . less energy expelled though, I presume.

March 30 at 11:38pm • Like

Anita Justine it was a spot only about the size of a dinner plate, it took about 5 minutes.

March 30 at 11:46pm • Like

Anita went from TMI to confused punctuation to WTMI (Wayyyy Too Much Information). Brava, Anita! And good job filling in the blanks in that last comment. Here's a li'l tip for the Anitas of the world: If you're telling a gross story, and the truth sounds bad, just LIE! No one needs to know that the pee spot was big enough to hypothetically fit a chicken thigh, a side of mashed potatoes, and some asparagus. When you put it that way, there's really no backing up your blow-dryer argument. The proper response to Justine's comment—regardless of truth—is "It only took 30 seconds." No further explanation needed.

AFTERWORD

Parents Doing It Right

S ometimes parents do it right. In fact, a *lot* of parents use social media in the ways that I believe it was intended to be used: To be funny and provide relatable entertainment for friends and family. Back when I first started the *STFU, Parents* blog, I began receiving submissions that weren't really categorized as "overshare," but I didn't want to toss them in the trash. After all, why only focus on the negative when the positive is so hilarious?

Parents who exercise their right to laugh at the trials of raising children are some of my very favorite people. They're able to take a frustrating situation and turn it into a funny one. Instead of acting like their children are precious gifts from God, they accept that no one is perfect, including their kids. This attitude allows them to transcend beyond the mundane gripes that come with parenting—like constant diaper changes, feedings, and baths—and craft truly entertaining jokes about their experiences. After running the blog for four months, I created the Mom's Gold Star, a reward for parents who use social media in a light and funny way.

Now, instead of just harping on about how parents suck at talking about their kids online, I can celebrate the parents who are doing it right. This chapter is my small way of saying thanks to all the funny parents out there who make my job a little less disgusting and make their friends' newsfeeds a lot more amusing.

 Luke When your wife says, "The baby just pooped," the correct response is not, "Wow, you're fucked."
August 30 at 6:56pm • Like • Comment

Luke learned a valuable lesson, and now he's passing that lesson on to his friends. Another helpful tip to dads: Don't call watching your kids while your wife is out "babysitting." It's not babysitting if they're *your* kids.

 Joan Two can cheat at Candyland, son. Two.
Sunday at 2:14pm via mobile • Like • Comment
👍 **15 people** likes this.

> **Connie** I refuse to play that game with Ethan anymore.
> Sunday at 2:37pm • Like 👍 1 person

> **Angie** Seth gets ugly near the peppermint forest.
> Sunday at 6:07pm • Like 👍 1 person

I know some people grew up with parents who were maybe a little *too* competitive with them—like parents who try to win at everything from I Spy and Hungry, Hungry Hippos to father-son basketball games—but most of the time, I think it's awesome when parents don't let their kids win at everything. Candy Land is some serious business, and the sooner kids wise up, the better. Joan's preschool-aged son thinks he can cheat at Candy Land and beat his own mom? Yeah. Right. Nice try, kid. Joan's onto you, and she's not afraid to knock your ass back to Lollipop Woods.

Rachel I'm pretty sure I just heard my husband whisper to the baby, "I could put your whole head in my mouth."

Monday at 9:22pm via mobile • Like • Comment

👍 **15 people** likes this.

> **Cynthia** Lol he totally could
> Monday at 9:23pm • Like 👍 1 person

Rachel gets my vote for "Parent I'd Most Like to Have as a Friend." Her status update is great not only for its humorous qualities, but for its awesome descriptive elements. I can totally picture her husband leaning over and whispering into the baby's ear like Bill Murray in *Lost in Translation*. In fact, from now on whenever I watch that movie I'm going to imagine that's what he says to Scarlett Johansson at the end. Maybe that's why she got so teary?

Sabina is amazed at how much work it is to suck, swallow, breathe.

8 hours ago via mobile • Like • Comment

👍 **3 people** likes this.

> **Erica** And takes sooo much coordination. How is he doing?
> 8 hours ago • Like

> **Courtney** Haven't you ever given a blo . . . never mind.
> 8 hours ago • Like

Valerie lmao^

8 hours ago • Like

Sabina So when I re-opened FB, I laughed at how open this post was for mis-interpretation (Thanks Courtney! . . . lol). I was talking about babies people . . . get your minds out of the gutter!

7 hours ago • Like

Although I find it hard to believe that Sabina didn't notice that "suck, swallow, breathe" is open to "misinterpretation," I think this thread is pretty damn funny. Kudos to Sabina for knowing how to take a joke and for having the types of friends who aren't afraid to be inappropriate at the expense of a newborn. A true friend will never shy away from a classic dirty joke.

Jared I just watched my child shove half of a cheeseburger in her mouth at once. It's like dining with a reticulated python.

21 minutes ago via mobile • Like • Comment

Jared is fascinated by (and possibly jealous of) the amount of food his daughter can consume at one time, which is sort of funny in itself, but the reticulated python joke takes it over the top. Now I'm picturing his daughter eating everything from cheeseburgers to whole rats to stray chickens.

Michelle "Please send a nut-free, milk-product-free, egg-free treat to school with your child to celebrate his/her birthday." Reeeeallly?

So I'm sending bourbon and cigarettes.

18 minutes ago via mobile • Like • Comment

👍 **9 people** like this.

Parenting today is made tougher by the fact that kids have so many allergies. It's nearly impossible to keep track of what's allowed in schools since the rules are always changing. Based on the list in Michelle's update, parents should be serving cucumber slices, raw ginger, flaxseed, and sprouts for their child's birthday. *Or,* as Michelle helpfully points out, bourbon and cigarettes, which was actually the preferred after-school snack for children in the '50s. I hope all the kids in Michelle's child's class like Maker's Mark!

Take the Quiz: "Do You Have What It Takes to Overshare?"

1. **Have you ever gleefully exclaimed out loud after receiving a high grade on a school paper?**
   a. I'm not the boastful type, so no. But I did stick every major assignment on the refrigerator and mentally high-five myself daily.
   b. Maybe a few times. I'm a bit of an overachiever, so it's hard to keep track of all my accomplishments.
   c. If I worked hard to earn that grade, you bet your ass I'm going to brag about it! Who rules the school?? THIS GUY!

2. **When you had sex for the first time, whom did you tell?**
   a. Only my best friend. But I also told her to tell our other eleven best friends.
   b. Just a few friends, the lady behind me at the grocery store, the postman, my grandma, and my German shepherd.

c. Who did I tell? Who *didn't* I tell?! I practically took out an ad in my local newspaper.

3. **Have you ever taken or wanted to take a picture of your food to share with friends?**
   a. Only the time that I ordered a massive "chocolate volcano" at the nicest restaurant in town. That thing was GOOD.
   b. Maybe, if what I'm eating looks appetizing. A bowl of chili doesn't make for the greatest photo.
   c. No meal is complete without a quick snapshot or five.

4. **What do you call your significant other when you're out in public?**
   a. Only by his/her first name, but we do have a tendency to grab each other's butts a lot.
   b. Usually a combination of pet names, but we try to keep them PG-rated.
   c. The same things we call each other when we're alone: "Mr. Holland's Opus" and "Mrs. Robinson."

5. **When people ask you how you're doing, what do you tell them?**
   a. I say, "I'm fine," and if they pry any further I get a little more specific.
   b. I tell the truth. If I'm having a bad day, I say so, but I may not elaborate too much on why.
   c. I launch into a twenty-minute tirade about my morning commute and why my car is a piece of crap. Sometimes I talk about why I'm pretty sure my husband is having an affair so I can get a second, third, or forty-fifth opinion.

6. **If a friend asks you how much you make for a living, what is your go-to answer?**
   a. I'll just indicate whether or not I'm comfortable with my current salary.
   b. I say something like, "Well, I bought that boat last year, how you do *think* I'm doing?!"
   c. I break down my exact salary, plus benefits and any stock options. I'm not shy about revealing my financial portfolio and I'm pretty impressed with myself.

7. **If you're suffering from an ailment or illness, how do you address the subject with your friends?**
   a. Unless it's serious, I may not tell my friends at all.
   b. I once confided in a few close friends about my toe fungus, but it was because it was sooo gross.
   c. All of my friends are acutely aware of my physical health and know my exact medications. I once sent an email to forty friends detailing a stint I had with food poisoning, including the number of times I puked. It was a little extreme, but *suuuper* funny.

8. **How do you convey to a dinner date that you need to use the bathroom?**
   a. I politely excuse myself and say that I'm going to the men's or women's room.
   b. I explain that I had a huge plate of nachos for lunch and my stomach is feeling a little unstable, *if you know what I mean.*
   c. I tell them I need to take a dump. After I return to the table I express utter delight that my bowels are relieved and describe whether the bathroom was dirty, since I assume they

want to know about the wet toilet paper on the floor. Who cares if we're eating?

9. **If you go on a diet and lose fifteen pounds, who do you tell?**
   a. I wait to see if anyone notices for a couple weeks. Then I start asking people how I look.
   b. I tell some friends because I know they'll be proud of me. Besides, I look *damn* good in a pair of form-fitting jeans, and my friends should acknowledge that.
   c. I tell pretty much everyone. Hey, I didn't starve myself for three months straight for nothing! I have no problem fishing for compliments, and if someone doesn't tell me what I want to hear, I really let 'em have it!

10. **What is your version of a reasonable birthday party for a one-year-old?**
    a. Invite some friends over on a Sunday afternoon, drink a few beers, and watch your baby cover herself in cake. Presents aren't a requirement, but I'm not exactly opposed to them!
    b. Organize a party and get a little upset when a few friends have conflicting plans scheduled for that date. Do they not understand what a milestone this is?
    c. Rent out an amusement park, arrange for a caterer, and register my baby at several high-end stores. My baby deserves THE BEST. And yes, that includes pony rides!

MOSTLY C'S: THE BORN OVERSHARER

As far as you're concerned, everything that happens in your day-to-day life should be shared with the world. When you have a baby, you will bombard your friends with pictures, fluid descriptions, and details about all the things you *think* they want to know, but don't.

This book could very well save you from yourself. Or at least save your friends from yourself.

MOSTLY B'S: THE OCCASIONAL OVERSHARER

Modesty runs in your family, but you're a bit of a loose cannon. When you have a baby, you'll probably keep the updates to a minimum until something significant happens, like a diaper blowout in the middle of a road trip. After that, all bets are off. This book will teach you how to stay in check no matter the circumstance.

MOSTLY A'S: THE WILD CARD

For the most part, you keep things to yourself. The chances that you'll overshare once you have a baby are slim, but that doesn't mean you're in the clear yet. Some of the worst offenders started out just like you—private, contemplative, and restrained—right up until little Paisley was born. Within seconds of her arrival, the world was shiny and new again, and *everything* had to be documented and posted online, from her first cry to her first bath to her first #2. In fact, someone who answers with Mostly As in this quiz could wind up being a bigger oversharer than someone with Mostly Cs if she/he isn't careful.

APPENDIX 2

STFU, Parents Bingo is based on the updates in your social media newsfeed(s). Fill up your scorecard by playing alone or with a group of people who share mutual friends that are known for oversharing. Just pull up the pages of those people whose status updates drive you crazy, and then mark each box based on recent status updates and photos.

Note: STFU, Parents Bingo can also be converted to a drinking game. But if you're doing a shot for every example of parent overshare you see these days, you'll probably wind up heavily intoxicated and unable to operate a motor vehicle within a few minutes. Just a warning.

STFU

PARENTS

BINGO

Mom's Gold Star	Daddy-jacking	Diaper Explosion	Cutest Baby Contest	Projectile Poop
Talking Fetus	Peanut Allergy	3D Sonogram	Mommy-jacking	Nap Time
Sancti-mommy	Momedy	★ STFU	Baby Barf	Merry Crapmas
Mucus Plug	Poop in the Potty	Nevaeh	Mama Drama	Double Wide Stroller
Natural Birth	Language Butchery	Woe Is Mom	Placenta Smoothie	Bath Poop

GLOSSARY

Here are some additional terms that you may encounter as you navigate the choppy waters of modern parenting culture.

Baby "Drop"
When you think of something dropping, here are a few things that might come to mind: the ball in Times Square on New Year's Eve, a sports player being dropped from a team, a carton of milk that somehow didn't make it back into the refrigerator properly, hip hop beats, and an unborn baby descending into a pregnant woman's pelvis a few weeks prior to labor. Oh wait, you don't normally think of that last one? Funny, because pregnant women on social media speak of it frequently! Did you know that when a baby "drops" in the womb it's also called "lightening"? As in, "I would rather be struck by lightning than listen to my friend talk about her lightening on Facebook"? It's true.

Birth Art (placenta prints, belly molds, etc.)
Birth art is a New Age concept that has trickled into the mainstream in recent years as parents obsess more and more about their perfect cre-

ations. Women attend workshops and retreats to get in touch with their inner goddess. They also make plaster belly casts at home using kits that include a selection of dazzling decorations. One of the most common types of birth art is a placenta print. You just take your bloody placenta, smoosh it onto some construction paper, and voilà! Art!

Birth Doll
Similar to birth art, knit birth dolls are all the rage. Birth dolls are scary educational dolls that often come with knit placentas and are meant to teach kids about the process of birth. They also make great chew toys for dogs.

Birth Junkie
If you own a birth doll and your lovingly hand-painted belly cast adorns the wall above your dining room table, you might be a birth junkie. You might also be a birth junkie if you fetishize the birth process, eat your placenta, and obsess over natural birth to the point of posting about it on social media and alienating friends who chose an epidural over a water birth. If you are a birth junkie, you may as well stop inviting non–birth junkie friends over for tea, because they're scared of what may you have put in it.

Brattleigh
A fancy word for a modern-day brat. "Brattleigh" is a joke that plays off the idea that parents add "leigh" to the end of baby names to make them yooneek [See *yooneek*.] If a random child is running around a restaurant unattended by her oblivious parents, you may feel inclined to give her the nickname Brattleigh. You may also feel inclined to trip the child as she runs by your table screaming for the fifteenth time, but it's highly unadvisable.

Code Brown
We all know what code brown means, right? It's a euphemism for taking a dump. My question is, why would any parent in his or her right

mind think it's funny to use "code brown" regarding their child in a status update? Especially if that code brown took place in an airplane or a restaurant booth? If there's one thing I don't want to think about when I'm traveling and/or enjoying a plate of pasta, it's another person's baby poop explosion. When you're giving your kid's poop nicknames and sharing them publicly to be funny, you may as well flush your friendships down the toilet.

Dadication

Today's dads will do whatever it takes to prove their commitment to their children. They will climb trees to retrieve ill-fated balloons. They will work overtime to ensure their kids get the best education. And they will mow down the guy who got the last Elmo doll in the Toys R Us parking lot with their Ford F-150s. And then they'll brag about it on Facebook. That's dadication.

Dadism

A dadism differs drastically from a momism. Where momisms are all over the map, dadisms tend to focus on one area in particular: nasty shit. Dads love coming up with crackerjack jokes about their kids pooping in their laps and their farts sounding into the next county. They get a kick out of projectile vomit shooting across the room, and their fatherly love often gets written in the form of, "Oh, *hail* yeah, my little girl just told me that she 'pooped out watermelon seeds!' I love my funny angel!" In short, dads almost always write about the same things on social media.

Diaper Blowout

A blowout is the cornerstone of parent overshare on social media. It can be defined as, "One of the grossest things a person will ever experience," but parents define it much more colorfully than that on Facebook (and I mean that literally—you can't talk about baby poop without talking about its color and texture, amirite?!). Babies typically have blowouts because they're constipated, and some babies get constipated regularly (no pun intended). Like a volcano, you never know when a baby's going to blow, and once he or she does, it's a giant, disgusting mess. No matter what happens, you better believe it's getting a mention, if not a full pictorial spread, on Facebook.

Dipe

The term "dipe" is momspeak for "diaper." It's a shortened version of the word, à la "hubs" and "hubby," and it is possibly the most annoying word in the history of made-up parenting slang. Every time a parent says "dipe" without irony, a baby has a blowout.

Documom

A documom is a mom who is addicted to documenting her kids' lives on social media. Whether it's with quotes, photos, or videos, documoms with smartphones are like junkies with an unlimited supply. They document every dental checkup, every bruise, every haircut, and even go so far as to post whole albums of surgeries. I've seen pictures of appendixes, tonsils, feeding tubes, and more.

Floater

This is the term used to describe what happens when constipated children take a warm bath. At least one in every five poop updates written by a parent on social media is about a floater, and yet every single one of them acts like it's the strangest, most rare occurrence in the history of bath time. Which is probably why so many of their status updates are accompanied by pictures.

Grrrr

The Woe Is Mom is not only a classy lady, she's also a *mom*. She tries not to curse too much on social media in order to preserve her new "mom" image, which works fine until she's super pissed off about something like the pool guy being twenty minutes late or the UPS guy waking up her baby. Instead of saying what she's really thinking, she'll let all her rage out on the "r" button and type "Grrrrr!!!!!!" Of course, we all know that anything more than four of the same letter or punctuation indicates that a person is thinking some pretty fucked-up stuff, but irritatingly, the "Grrrr" mom never breaks character.

Lactation Cookies
Unlike breast milk cheese, lactation cookies are a recipe for helping breastfeeding women increase their milk supply, as opposed to cookies actually made with breast milk. They're pretty much just cookies made with oats, yeast, and flaxseed. No bodily fluids required! If your friend discusses eating them on social media, you can rest assured that she is not eating herself.

Liquid Gold
This is the name ascribed to breast milk because it is apparently the answer to all of life's problems. In fact, if world leaders would just come together for a slice of Key lime pie and each drink a few ounces of liquid gold, we could eliminate the strife among nations! Who says oil is liquid gold? Not moms! It's breast milk that's the real cure-all for everything from pinkeye and diaper rash to famine and religious persecution! Look it up. The antibodies are extremely potent.

LOL and LMFAO
"Laugh out loud" (LOL), "laughing my ass off" (LMAO), and "laughing my fucking ass off" (LMFAO) are all commonly used Internet acronyms used by parents when they post about something that usually isn't funny at all, like being handed a piece of poop by their toddler son or being vomited on by their infant daughter. If you're a parent who's tempted to use "LOL" as a way to cushion your status update about the nasty side of parenting, you're probably better off erasing your update altogether. Because it's not funny.

Mama Bear
The term "mama bear" has been used for ages but became popularized when Sarah Palin talked about mama grizzlies protecting their cubs by

attacking people who pose a threat. Since then, women have used "Don't mess with the mama bear!" as an excuse to do everything from gossiping to hair pulling to face beating in the unfortunate instance that another adult or child looks at her "cub" the wrong way.

Momarazzi

The momarazzi describes moms who take so many pictures of their kids that they have a new album for every day, week, or month of their lives. They're documoms who specialize in photos of everyday life, like bath time or playtime or naptime. Momarazzis can't even determine which pictures are worth posting on Facebook anymore because they have hundreds and hundreds to choose from. You'd think they were getting paid to take so many pictures after looking through an album of two-hundred-plus pictures of a baby eating peas in a high chair. Their photo albums look like stills from a movie, shot with a high-definition camera so that every bit of drool gets captured for high-definition memories. They are the visual definition of overshare.

Mombie

A mombie is a woman who "changes" after having a baby. She's been brainwashed by motherhood, but she's practically oblivious to the changes, like an inability to hold a conversation without going into detail about poop explosions or pacifier recalls. Through dead, sleepless eyes, her one and only focus is on her baby, and while zombies tend to chow down on brains, a mombie is more inclined to gnaw on a piece of placenta. She loves nothing more than joining an army of other mombies, so don't be surprised if your old friend-turned-mombie begins to spend her time primarily with other mombies who are all covered in some kind of murky baby secretion. She may return to her old self one day, but it could take months or even years for that to happen.

Mombie's Law

Like Murphy's Law, which states that, "Anything that can go wrong will go wrong," Mombie's Law assumes that any status update that can be mommyjacked will be mommyjacked. This is why there are multiple forms of mommyjacking, including deathjacking, non-sequiturjacking, and petjacking. The times when you least expect to be mommyjacked are actually the times you should most expect it.

Momism
Unlike dadisms, which are usually about farts and teaching kids how to poop outside, momisms tend to include naptime complaints, arguments that stay-at-home moms should be paid an annual salary of $50,000 to $120,000, and the occasional rant about how difficult it is to grocery shop when you're stopped every five feet because your baby is just so damn adorable. There's no statistical data to back me up, but I'm fairly certain that momisms are as boring as pictures of food, except with more sanctimony.

Nevaeh
Climbing the charts in popularity as well as becoming the number one most annoying name in America, Nevaeh is "Heaven" spelled backward. Like I said. Name drama.

P.O.B.
P.O.B. stands for "pack of bitches." There's always a pack of bitches lurking on Facebook, waiting to pounce on an innocent poster making a casual observation. Most P.O.B.s are moms attacking other moms or unhelpfully trying to be helpful, for example, when a pregnant woman says she isn't getting much sleep, and a P.O.B. comes along to tell her to enjoy her sleep now, because once the baby is here she'll *never sleep again* until the child is old enough to vote. P.O.B.s are the grown-up, bitter mom versions of mean girls in junior high. They can often be found comparing Woe Is Mom tales at Starbucks on Saturday mornings.

Poopy Diaper Game (baby shower)
The Poopy Diaper Game is one the grossest inventions of our time. It's a baby shower game that consists of melting different types of chocolate

bars in diapers and then asking, nay, *forcing* baby shower guests to guess which one is which. Probably the worst part about the game is the waste of perfectly good chocolate bars, with the second-worst part being imagining eating them out of baby diapers.

PTBPD (post-traumatic birth picture disorder)
PTBPD is a condition that social media users may get after viewing a graphic selection of birth photos. Post-traumatic birth picture disorder afflicts thousands of innocent social media users every single day. In fact, one of the highest-paying jobs in the year 2030 will be "social media therapist" due to all of the PTBPD flashbacks, not to mention years of increased online birth pictures exposure. There will be a whole generation of children growing up and discovering old pictures of themselves sitting naked in a crib full of feces, clutching a partially chewed-up birth doll.

Pumping
Things that can be pumped: tires, balloons, wells, Reebok Pumps, lactating breasts. Which one would you feel the least comfortable reading about on a nightly basis? (Hint: If you say Reebok Pumps, you are *wrong, wrong, wrong.*)

Push Present
A push present is a gift that a father gives to a mother after she gives birth to their child. Sure, the real "gift" is a screaming, healthy baby, but what kind of present is *that*? Despite being shiny and new, a newborn will never be as shiny as an expensive piece of jewelry or a new car. It will never appreciate like a piece of art or shimmer like an in-ground pool. These days, if you expect a woman to carry a baby for forty weeks, you better make plans to hand her the keys to something wrapped in a big red bow that comes with a four-cylinder turbocharged engine, ergonomic cabin seating, and three-zone automatic climate control.

SAHM

The acronym for "stay-at-home mom." It's associated with many things (vodka before noon, Juicy sweatsuits, Farmville, and baby picture–spamming on Facebook), and its definition is constantly being redefined decade by decade. In the '50s, you had Donna Reed; in the '70s, you had Carol Brady; and in 2013, you have the Real Housewives. All highly influential figures in the lives of SAHMs.

Skullet

A skullet is a baby mullet. It is often the result of a baby's hair loss before the age of six months and can be defined as "a baby in the front with a party in the back." It's similar to the look middle-aged men sport when they have no hair on top and a ponytail in the back, minus the desperation.

Speashol Czsnoflayke

Children today are special snowflakes who aren't allowed to play in dirt, jump off high dives, or touch anything without being smothered in antibacterial gel. They are entertained by the fanciest gadgets on the market, but they don't know how to tie their own shoes. They have refined palates and prefer sushi to goldfish crackers. Most significantly, they are told that they are the best at everything. Did you know it's possible for a child to be the best at playing with LEGOs?

Sprinkle

Some women have low-key baby showers (usually for a second baby) that are affectionately and obnoxiously called "sprinkles." Rather than have a big shower, a woman's friends will "sprinkle" her with gifts. It is the smaller, "encore" wedding of the baby shower world.

TMI

An acronym that stands for "too much information." Being called out for posting something that's TMI is like being accused of farting in an elevator. It's a shorthand way of saying, "For the love of God, please keep that to yourself."

VBAC
VBAC stands for "vaginal birth after Caesarean"—four words that should never appear together in a status update for any reason. And yet, they do.

Wambulance
When a Woe Is Mom is having a breakdown, she's in dire need of a fictional ambulance otherwise known as the "wambulance." The wambulance is almost like a paddywagon for whiners who have "first-world problems" and need to be pampered out of their misery. If a Woe Is Mom complains that construction crews remodeling her bathroom are waking up her toddler, she should probably take a seat on the wambulance.

Yooneek/Yoonique
William Shakespeare once wrote, "What's in a name? That which we call a rose by any other name would smell as sweet." I think today's parents take that sentiment literally, focusing all their efforts on giving their children unique, and often yooneekly spelled, names that they think will set them apart from their classmates, coworkers, and potential running mates throughout life. Unfortunately, this plan usually backfires, but that isn't going to stop modern parents from trying! You can't have a Speashol Czsnoflayke without a name like Bently Jamyz Messiah.

ACKNOWLEDGMENTS

First and foremost, I owe a great deal of gratitude to social media technology, without which we wouldn't know the human capacity to overshare on the Internet. Thank you to all of the blog readers, commenters, and submitters for being hilarious and supportive, and for taking the time to read *STFU, Parents* out of a zillion other blogs. Many thanks to my agent, Kent D. Wolf, for having faith in me; my editor, Meg Leder, for being sharp and enthusiastic; and to the rest of the team at Perigee/Penguin for helping me achieve a blogger's dream come true.

Thanks to Darcy Reenis for designing the *STFU, Parents* logo, and for continued mutual support and friendship. Proper respect to Karyn Spencer for her encouragement and savviness, and to Kristyn Pomranz for her mentor-like role in my blogging "career." Shout-outs to Sarah B. Head for always knowing what to say; my brother, Mike Koenig, for keeping it real; and all of my friends and relatives who actually read and enjoy the blog. I'm honored and embarrassed to entertain you guys with pictures of placenta.

A very heartfelt thank-you goes to my parents, Harvey and Marsha Koenig, who have long suffered through my endless phone calls and who are truly my biggest champions. They taught me everything I know, so if you have a problem with me, blame them. Additionally, thanks to all of the oversharing parents out there, especially if they pick up this book and think it's funny. And last but not least, thanks to my main man, Brian Blessinger, without whom I could not have written the blog or book. Just ask him. He'll tell you. He's been scarred for life, and we don't even have kids yet.

ABOUT THE AUTHOR

Photo by Michael Sofronski

Blair Koenig is a Brooklyn-based writer and humorist. In 2009, she created the blog *STFU, Parents*, which is now an entertainment destination for thousands of daily readers. Blair has been on *Good Morning America*, *Today*, and *The Ricki Lake Show*; and *STFU, Parents* has been featured in many outlets including the *Huffington Post*, the *Washington Post*, MSNBC, *Salon*, *Slate*, *Babble*, *Parenting*, and *Mommyish*, where Blair writes a weekly column. The blog has been called "a breath of sanity in a sea of braggadocio and TMI," and Blair is often told that she's performing a valuable public service. She has yet to file for 501(c)(3) tax exemption status.

STFUParentsBlog.com
@STFUParents
www.facebook.com/STFUParents